Mind over
Back Pain

Mind over Back Pain

A Radically New Approach to the Diagnosis and Treatment of Back Pain

by JOHN SARNO, M.D.

William Morrow and Company, Inc.
New York 1984

Library of Congress Catalog Card Number: 84-60564

ISBN: 0-688-02863-2

RD
768
.S27
1984

Printed in the United States of America

2 3 4 5 6 7 8 9 10

BOOK DESIGN BY PATTY LOWY

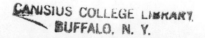

Acknowledgments

Though the writing of this book was started a number of years ago, the fact that it has become a reality is primarily due to the interest, encouragement and activity of Michael Shimkin. He was the prime mover in setting the publication wheels in motion. He has also been of great help in reading and critiquing the manuscript as it developed.

My wife, Martha, as always, has contributed to the project in many ways. From her considerable medical writing experience, she made suggestions ranging from organization to syntax. Her sensitivity to psychological phenomena made her an ideal discussant as I worked to clarify concepts.

David Schechter, while still a third-year medical student, collected the data that comprise the follow-up study reported in the text. In addition, he made excellent suggestions after multiple readings of the manuscript.

Howard A. Rusk has been many things to me over the years. He is the philosophical father of the medical specialty of Rehabilitation Medicine. He introduced me to the field, and was a constant source of support and encouragement during the years that I worked under his departmental chairmanship. Because of his clinical sensitivity and deep understanding of patient needs, he was particularly supportive of my work on back pain.

The many workers who have contributed to the field of psychosomatic medicine are too numerous to list, but one thinks with particular gratitude of a few pioneers such as Franz Alexander, Flanders Dunbar and George Engel.

Acknowledgments

I would be remiss if I did not acknowledge the contributions of the members of the team at the Institute of Rehabilitation Medicine who worked with me through the years in the treatment of patients. They have been devoted, sensitive and caring. In particular I am grateful to Arlene Feinblatt, the chief psychologist of our group, for her contribution to the understanding of the psychological basis for the tension myositis syndrome and to Roberta Weiss, Phyllis Israelton and Nancy Berk for their work in developing appropriate physical therapeutic techniques.

I owe thanks as well to my patients, for they have been the textbooks from whom I have learned about this disorder.

I am particularly grateful to Cinda Firestone for her gracious and generous support of the back pain program. She also kindly consented to read the manuscript and in the process made many valuable suggestions.

Elizabeth Frost Knappman made important organizational suggestions at a crucial time in the writing of the book, for which I am very grateful.

To Mary Bleecker Simmons goes the credit for the title of the book.

Finally, my thanks for the loyalty and industriousness of Ana Torres, who typed the seemingly endless pages that led to the final manuscript.

Contents

Mind over
Back Pain

Introduction

Back pain has reached epidemic proportions in the Western world. It is one of the most common disorders for which people seek medical help. It is also the single largest cause of worker absenteeism in the United States, Sweden, Great Britain and Canada, accounting for billions of dollars each year in medical costs.[1] Perhaps 80 to 90 percent of Americans experience pain in the neck, shoulder or back during their lifetime. At the least, such pain is temporarily annoying; more often than not, it produces qualitative changes in people's lives. Victims may be unable to participate in leisure-time activities, or worse, they are significantly restricted in their daily work.

Clearly, this is a phenomenon of the twentieth century. Why? And how has this come to pass? At a time when medical science presents us with such impressive accomplishments, why has it been unable to solve this common problem?

This book supports the idea that this great problem exists because the medical community has failed to recognize the major cause of back pain. Medical writings on the back routinely attribute pain to various structural abnormalities of the spine. In this book I shall endeavor to show that it is actually tension that causes most back pain.

I first appreciated the magnitude of the problem of back pain in 1965 when I joined the staff of the Institute of Rehabilitation Medicine at New York University Medical Center as director of outpatient services. For the first time in my medical career I began to see large numbers of patients with neck, shoulder, back and buttock pain. I had received conventional medical training and was under the impression that pain in these locations was due to a variety of structural abnormalities of the spine, most commonly arthritis and disc disorders, or to a vague group of muscle conditions thought to be due to poor posture, weakness, overexertion and the like. I believed that pain in the legs or arms indicated nerve involvement and was a sign of a spinal structural aberration. However, I was not sure how any of these abnormalities actually produced the pain.

The rationale for the treatment I prescribed was equally perplexing. Occasionally I would inject a painful area with a local anesthetic, with mixed results. In almost every case physical therapy was prescribed, consisting of ultrasound treatment to bring heat to the muscles, as well as massage and exercise. No one was sure what these procedures were supposed to do, but they seemed to help in some cases. It was said that the exercise strengthened the abdominal and back muscles and that this somehow supported the spine and prevented pain.

I found the experience of treating back pain frustrating and depressing, for I could never predict the outcome. Furthermore, I became increasingly troubled by the fact that the pattern of the patient's pain and the findings on physical examination could rarely be satisfactorily explained by the presumed pathology. For example, pain might be attributed to degenerative arthritis of the joints of the last lumbar vertebra (spinal bone). But the patient often had pain in places that had nothing to do with this bone.

Gradually I began to doubt the accuracy of the conventional diagnoses and at the same time to realize that the pain appeared to be coming from something that was happening in the muscles of the neck, shoulders or back. Throughout this transitional period I continued to treat with physical therapy, with generally unsatisfactory results, though some patients did very well. I began to think, however, that the outcome had more to do with how patients related to me than the treatment I prescribed.

When it became obvious to me that the pain was coming from something going on in the muscles, another important piece was added to the puzzle. Studies revealed that most patients with back pain (it turned out to be 88 percent) had a history of such things as tension or migraine headache, heartburn or stomach ulcer, colitis, spastic colon, allergies and a few less common disorders, all of which are related to tension, so I concluded that this painful muscle condition might also be due to tension. When that theory was put to the test and patients were treated accordingly, there was an obvious improvement in the results of treatment. In fact, it was possible now to predict which patients would do well and which might not.

At that point the exact nature of the painful process in the muscles was still not clear, though muscle spasm was one of the elements. It was apparent that nervous tension initiated the process. But what kind of change did it produce in the muscle, and how did the nerves get involved?

A combination of further patient observation and a search of the medical literature suggested to me that tension affected the circulation of blood to the involved areas and that when muscles and their associated nerves were deprived of their normal supply of blood, the result was pain in the back and/or limbs. Specifically, a reduction in local blood supply resulted in reduced oxygen to the muscles and nerves, which appeared to be the direct cause of muscle and nerve pain.

Later the work of two German scientists, Dr. H. G. Fassbender and Dr. K. Wegner, came to my attention. They obtained biopsies from the muscles of patients with back pain and studied the tissue under the electron microscope. This type of microscope is capable of far greater magnification than the usual type and permits the study of the inside of cells. They found changes in muscle cells that suggested oxygen deprivation.[2] Their work supported the idea that reduced levels of oxygen in involved muscles is the cause of back pain.

What does the medical world think of this diagnosis? First, it is unlikely that most physicians are aware of it. I have written a number of medical papers and chapters for textbooks on the subject, but they have reached a limited medical audience—primarily physicians and those in other disciplines working in the field of physical medicine and rehabilitation. However, judging by the reaction of doctors in my immediate medical environment, most physicians have either ignored or rejected the concept. Many doctors in my own specialty see the validity of the diagnosis but find it difficult to treat such patients. This is related directly to the fact that the disorder is not purely "physical." Most doctors are uncomfortable with medical conditions that have a psychological basis. However, increasing numbers of doctors in the United States, particularly in the younger generations of physicians, are beginning to appreciate the important role of emotions in health and illness, especially the role of stress in clinical disorders. It is my hope that this book will be an inspiration to them to learn more about this disorder.

What of the readers with a history of back pain? It is not my intention to diagnose and treat in this book. Though the syndromes of neck, shoulder and back pain are not inherently complicated, they require individual attention. I shall describe my experience with a large number of patients over many years in the hope that the reader can extract something helpful from this experience. However, the larger problem will not be solved until there is a change in the general medical perception of the cause of back pain.

Science requires that all new ideas be validated by experimentation and replication. Before new concepts can be generally accepted they must be proven beyond all doubt. It is essential, therefore, that the ideas advanced in this book be subjected to research study. Because of my own successful experience in treating back pain, I am confident that research will bear me out, to the advantage of everyone suffering from the crippling effects of back pain.

Chapter 1
Structural Abnormalities Rarely Cause Back Pain

What do you think of when you first feel pain in the neck, shoulder or back? "I knew I shouldn't have raked those leaves yesterday (or washed the car, or done the laundry, or painted the ceiling)." "It must have been that fall on the ice last week (or last month, or last year)." "I've been running too much (playing tennis too much, bowling too much)."

Most people think that they must have hurt themselves somehow, and in some cases pain does begin after a traumatic physical incident, so the idea of injury seems logical. Patients often say, "I'm afraid of hurting myself again, so I'm going to be very careful in what I do."

These ideas have been fostered by the medical profession and other disciplines, for they have always assumed that neck, shoulder and back (including buttock) pain is due to injury or disease of the spine and associated structures; but contrary to popular belief, injuries or diseases of the spine are rarely responsible for the common neck, shoulder or backache. However, the idea that the pain is due to a variety of structural abnormalities of the spine is so deeply ingrained in medical thinking that alternative diagnoses are rarely considered in current practice.

What is the explanation for medicine's preoccupation with the spine? Since the late nineteenth century, medical thinking and training have been largely mechanical and structural in orientation. The body has been viewed as an exceedingly complex machine, and illness has been interpreted as malfunction in the machine brought about by many different factors, some of which come from outside the body, such as infection or trauma, some based on inherited defects and some caused by the degeneration of various organs and systems. But there has been limited awareness of the possible role of emotions in both illness or health until recently. The majority of practicing physicians today do not generally consider that emotions play a significant role in causing physical disorders, though many would acknowledge that emotions might aggravate a physically caused illness. Many physicians feel uncomfortable in dealing with a medical problem that is related to psychological factors.

A good example is the peptic ulcer. It has been known for many years that ulcers are caused by tension, but the primary focus in treatment has always been "medical" and not "psychological." Drugs are prescribed to neutralize excessive acid in the stomach or, if possible, prevent its secretion. Although this is a perfectly reasonable thing to do, it would seem logical to put the major focus of treatment on the cause of the problem and work with the patient to reduce the tension somehow. Physicians prefer that psychiatrists handle emotions, and physical doctors handle "medical" problems. Therefore, in the case of stomach ulcers the basic *cause* of the disorder can go without proper attention.

Considering this long medical tradition, it is not surprising that without real evidence, pain syndromes of the neck, shoulders, back and buttocks continue to be interpreted as structural in origin.

If structural abnormalities don't cause pain in the neck, shoulders and back in most cases, what does? That, of course, is the subject of this book.

Briefly, my studies and clinical experience of the past eighteen years suggest that these pains are brought on by tension. Among most victims of back pain, tension leads to a physical process involving the muscles and nerves of the neck, shoulders and back. I call this condition the *tension myositis syndrome* (TMS).[1,2] Though the suffix *itis* usually refers to inflammation, it is used here to designate a change of state in muscle *(myo)*. The change is circulatory; tension constricts the blood vessels feeding the involved muscles, and the resultant blood deprivation leads to painful muscle spasm and nerve pain.

TMS is characterized by varied patterns of pain in the neck, shoulders, upper or lower back and often in the legs and arms as well. Pain can recur with increasing frequency over many years, and in some people it eventually becomes chronic. It can dominate a person's life. Pain and the fear of pain sharply restrict physical activity. This can vary from simple actions such as putting on one's shoes to more complex activities such as participation in sports. Victims feel inadequate as a parent or spouse since they can't play with the children, can't sit long enough to attend a movie, can't entertain, can't even enjoy sex. The breadwinner worries about the family financial situation, job security, etc. The wife feels guilty about not being a good wife or mother.

All these consequences of TMS produce more anxiety; they increase internal tension and perpetuate the pain-producing process. Patients become apprehensive, worried, frustrated and depressed. They often feel alone and isolated and think their situation is unique. Some patients spend small fortunes on consultations and long treatment, willing to try anything that might bring relief.

Worst of all, fear is the back pain patient's constant companion: fear of physical deterioration (''my spine is degenerating''), fear of further injury to the back (''my disc will herniate again''), fear of disability, fear of cancer. And in addition there is fear of the pain itself, particularly the severe, excruciating attacks of spasm that are so common.

All this is particularly unfortunate because TMS is generally harmless physically. It rarely leads to significant damage to the nerves involved and never to the muscles. It is not a disease or a malignancy. The severity of the pain is out of proportion to the condition causing it because the process is benign in the same way a severe leg cramp is benign. The fear engendered creates a vicious cycle.

Before proceeding to a description of TMS and its treatment, let us look at the conventional diagnoses.

THE DIAGNOSIS OF HERNIATED DISC

What are discs? They are nature's shock absorbers, placed between all the spinal bones to ease the impact of the body weight on them. They are poorly named because they are not independent units that can pop in and out of place. Therefore, the term "slipped disc" is a poor description of what occurs. A disc is like a tough sleeve connecting the bodies of two vertebrae and filled with a thick fluid that absorbs the shock of normal back movement. The discs at the lower end of the spine (lumbar) are subject to a lot of stress, and the sleeve often begins to wear out quite early in life. When this occurs, the fluid may bulge at a weak point or actually break through. The latter is called a ruptured or herniated disc. It is routinely blamed for the leg pain known as sciatica.

The diagnosis of a herniated disc is often made solely on the basis of a history of simultaneous low back (including buttock) and/or leg pain. In many of these cases plain X rays of the spine show narrowing of a lower lumbar disc space, which is seen as evidence that the disc has degenerated. This may be seen on any X ray of an adult, though it becomes more common as one gets older. But neither the location of the pain nor the evidence of a degenerated disc on X ray are proof that there is a herniation. In fact, a disc in the advanced stages of degeneration cannot herniate, for there is probably very little fluid left. To make such a diagnosis without appropriate evidence, with all the apprehension that it arouses, is irresponsible.

Of greater importance, however, is the fact that even a proven herniated disc *does not cause pain* in the majority of cases. Here are the reasons why.

I have successfully treated many patients who had documented lumbar herniated discs—that is, they had either positive myelograms or CT scans.* My treatment could not have been successful had the patients' pain been due to disc herniation. In most cases symptoms had been present for months, sometimes years, and had resisted all treatment attempts. One could only conclude that the herniated disc was not the cause of the pain. By treating for TMS with success, the point was proven.

I have also seen a number of disc surgery operative reports in which it is clear that the disc herniation did not compress the nearby nerve. It is not correct to assume, therefore, that a disc herniation will compress a spinal nerve.

Finally, I have treated patients in whom disc herniation *was* found to be compressing a spinal nerve at surgery but who continued to have precisely the same pain after the disc material was removed. These patients turned out to have TMS and thus responded to my treatment. My conclusion was that the disc abnormality was not causing the pain.

There is additional evidence that attributing back and leg pain to disc herniation is often incorrect.

Figure 1 shows how spinal nerves peel off the spinal cord at every level, one on each side of the body. In the lumbar area (the lower area) these nerves are bound for the legs, where they bring messages from the brain to move leg muscles. They also bring sensory messages from the legs to the brain, such as pain and other sensations, including the position of the legs and their parts. The spinal nerves do not go directly into the legs but send branches to what are called peripheral nerves, such as the sciatic, as seen in the drawing. However, in Figures 2 and 3 you will see that there is a distinct sensory area in each leg that is served

---

*A myelogram is a special X-ray study in which dye is introduced into the spinal canal, outlining the spinal cord and spinal nerves as they take off from the cord. If a disc is herniated it can be seen on this X ray. A CT scan is a new X-ray technique that gives information not available on regular X rays, through computerization. A CT scan can show a herniated disc.

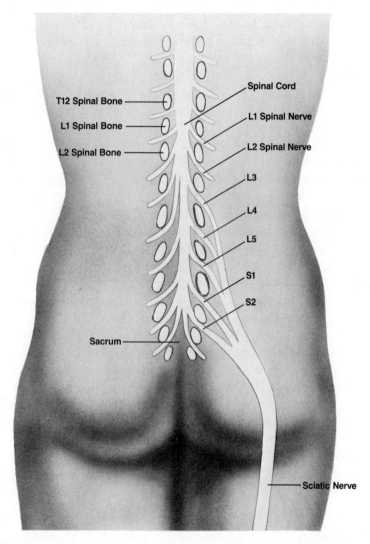

Figure 1. **A drawing of the lower back showing the spinal nerves and how they contribute to the formation of sciatic nerves**

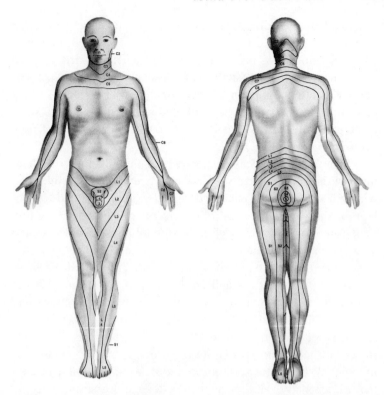

Figures 2 & 3. **Two drawings of what is known as the dermatone distribution of the spinal nerves over the body—that is, the specific parts of the body served by each spinal nerve, carrying sensory messages from the body to the spinal cord and then to the brain**

by each spinal nerve. Note that L1 serves the groin area, L2 the upper thigh, etc.

Now let us suppose there is a herniated disc pressing on the L5 spinal nerve to the left leg. It can be seen readily from Figure 2 where the person should feel pain in the leg. I have often seen patients who came with that diagnosis, herniated disc at L5. However, instead of having pain only in the restricted area shown in the drawing, they had pain over the L2, L3, L4, L5 and S1 portions of the leg, thus indicating that the pain could not be due to a herniated disc at L5. Since the sciatic nerve is made up of branches from L3, L4, L5, S1 and S2, as shown in Figure 1, the pain could have been the result of something irritating the sciatic nerve. This is exactly what is seen with TMS. Such patients will often complain of occasional pain in the opposite leg as well, pain that cannot be attributed to a herniated disc, since discs generally herniate to one side only. *Involvement of both sides is common with TMS.*

Here is a typical case history of a patient diagnosed as having a herniated lumbar disc. He was a twenty-five-year-old man with a history of low back and right leg pain who had a myelogram showing a herniated disc two months before I saw him in consultation. He was advised to stop all physical activity, and surgery was recommended. He was devastated by the diagnosis, since vigorous sports, such as basketball and squash, had always been an important and enjoyable part of his life. He described himself as sensitive and excessively conscientious and had found that athletics were essential to burn off his tension.

It is a testament to his courage (and perhaps his reluctance to accept the diagnosis) that he refused surgery and, with great trepidation, began to work out in a gymnasium and play basketball occasionally. He got neither better nor worse but lived in fear of a recurrence of severe pain.

The physical examination on the day of the consultation disclosed no evidence of nerve damage in either leg. The straight leg raising test on both sides caused pain in the right buttock. There was also pain on pressure over the muscles of the sides of the neck, top of the shoulders and both buttocks.

The history and physical findings indicated that the pain was due to TMS and not a herniated disc. He accepted the diagnosis, participated in the treatment program and became symptom-free in a few weeks. He has been doing well since (twenty-eight months later, at the time of writing) and has resumed all his usual vigorous athletic activities.

One can ignore the presence of a herniated disc in this manner only if there is evidence that something else may be causing the pain. If one treats the patient for TMS and he gets better and, most importantly, stays better the TMS diagnosis has been vindicated.

THE DIAGNOSIS OF "PINCHED NERVE"

Although the low back, buttocks and legs are the most common locations for TMS, it often occurs in the neck, shoulders and arms. Usually this is not as frightening as low back and leg pain, but it can be very painful and disabling. The usual structural diagnosis for this is "pinched nerve." It is assumed that one of the spinal nerves emerging in the neck, as seen in Figure 4, is compressed by a bone spur from one of the cervical vertebrae.

There are a few things that cast doubt on this diagnosis. First, it fails to explain why this kind of pain occurs in young adults before they develop bone spurs, making that diagnosis untenable.

Second, bone spurs are extremely common, and most people who have them don't have pain. Spurs increase in number and size with advancing age, so that by late middle age and beyond everyone ought to have neck and arm pain from them, but they don't.

Finally, I have been informed by specialists experienced in reading X rays of the nervous system that it would take a very large spur to compress a spinal nerve in the neck. This is rarely seen in X rays of patients who have neck, shoulder and arm pain. On the other hand, it has been reported in the medical literature that even large growths in the neck, such as benign tumors, often produce no pain.[3]

What is the alternative to this diagnosis? TMS commonly involves the muscles and nerves of the neck and shoulders. Figure 4 shows this area, including the nerve network known as the *brachial plexus*. It is here that spinal nerves from the neck are organized and send branches to the peripheral nerves going to the arms and hands. TMS in this region may involve muscles,

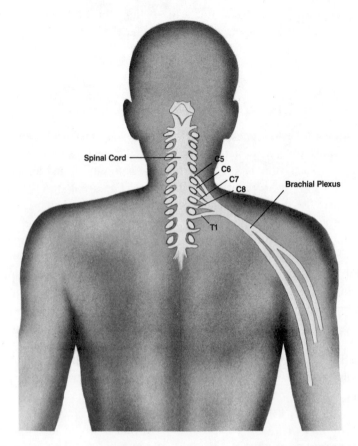

Spinal Cord

C5
C6
C7
C8

Brachial Plexus

T1

Figure 4. **A drawing of the neck and shoulders showing the cervical spinal nerves and how they go to make up the brachial plexus. TMS often involves the brachial plexus, which means that the patient will have pain, numbness or tingling in the arms or hands**

spinal nerves or parts of the brachial plexus, resulting in neck and shoulder pain, as well as pain, numbness and tingling somewhere in the arms and/or hands. Numbness and tingling are symptoms of oxygen deprivation of nerves and are very common with TMS.

OTHER STRUCTURAL DIAGNOSES

A number of other structural diagnoses are made in response to back pain. Here are some of the most common diagnoses.

Arthritis in the joints of the spine is a feature of the normal aging process. Arthritic changes often begin in early adulthood. Though frequently cited as the cause of neck or back pain, I have not found that this is the case. It is, however, a convenient explanation for pain that is otherwise undiagnosed.

Transitional vertebra, spina bifida occulta and *spondylolysis* are congenital abnormalities in bone structure at the lower end of the spine. All are easily seen on X ray and are often blamed for pain, but none has ever been responsible for pain in patients I have examined and treated. This is supported by a medical paper published by Dr. C. A. Splithoff, a radiologist; the paper appeared in the *Journal of the American Medical Association* in 1953. Splithoff compared the occurrence of nine different abnormalities of the lower end of the spine in patients with and without back pain.[4] He concluded that patients *without* backache demonstrated structural aberrations just as frequently as patients with back pain, thus suggesting that back pain could not be attributed to these nine structural abnormalities.

More recently, Drs. A. Magora and A. Schwartz of Israel have been conducting a similar study. They have shown that just as many people without back pain have osteoarthritis of the lumbar spine, transitional vertebrae, spina bifida occulta and spondylolysis as those with back pain.[5,6,7,8]

Scoliosis is an abnormal curvature of the spine commonly found in teenage girls and usually persisting into adult life. Its cause is unknown. Scoliosis rarely causes pain in teenagers but is often blamed for back pain in adults. I have never found this to be the case in patients I have treated, one of whom is exemplified in the following case history.

The patient was a thirty-five-year-old housewife who had

suffered recurrent attacks of back pain since her teens. Five years before the date of her consultation with me she experienced a severe attack at a period in her life when she was taking care of a newborn baby and a two-year-old child. X rays showed mild scoliosis, and the pain was attributed to this. She was told that her back pain would gradually get worse as she got older.

The patient recovered from that episode and did fairly well until about two months before I saw her, when she had a recurrence of severe pain. She said it began when she was bending over and "felt something snap." This is a common description of onset and invariably suggests to patients that something terrible has happened to their back, though we know in retrospect that this is not the case. The pain continued to be severe, accompanied by tilting of the trunk to one side.

In addition to the history of recurrent back pain, the patient reported a great deal of tendinitis in her arms and legs, occasional pain in the neck and shoulders and episodes of both stomach and colon symptoms, hay fever and severe headaches for many years. These are typical of people who are likely to develop back pain due to TMS and reflect a tense personality.

The physical examination was essentially normal except that she was unable to bend and had pain on pressure over the neck, shoulder, upper back and buttock muscles.

The patient participated in the treatment program for TMS with prompt disappearance of her symptoms. She reported in a telephone interview twenty-one months after the completion of treatment that she had had no further difficulty with her back. She was aware that she might have mild neck, shoulder or back pain in the future, but she knew that it was a benign process and that she could expect rapid, spontaneous resolution of these symptoms.

This patient's spinal abnormality was not the source of her pain, since the scoliosis was unchanged by the treatment. It is equally clear that she had a propensity for expressing excess tension physically, as so many of us do. To confuse these is a diagnostic tragedy.

Spondylolisthesis refers to a malalignment at the lower end of the spine that is commonly said to cause low back pain. I have had a number of patients with this abnormality and have found in each case that the patient also had TMS. In every case the pain was eliminated by appropriate treatment for TMS, suggesting that spondylolisthesis was not the cause. Here is a dramatic case history.

The patient was a fifty-eight-year-old businessman who had been having increasingly severe low back pain for about three years when I first examined him. He had consulted a number of excellent physicians in New York during that time—all of whom recommended surgery, particularly as the pain became increasingly severe. When I saw him he was in a state of great turmoil. The pain was ruining his life. He had been an enthusiastic tennis player for many years and missed this enjoyable outlet for his tension very much. His days at the office were torture, and his worry and concern over the problem affected both his professional and his personal life.

On examination he exhibited no neurological changes—that is, the reflexes in his legs, his muscle strength and his sensory function were all normal. Whatever was causing his pain was not seriously affecting any of the nerves in his back or buttocks. On the other hand, virtually all his back muscles were painful on palpation.

It was very clear to me that in addition to the spondylolisthesis he had severe tension myositis and that this probably was responsible for his pain. When I discussed this with him he told me that he wanted desperately to believe me since he wished to avoid surgery but couldn't understand how all these physicians could be wrong. I pointed out they were not wrong, that the spondylolisthesis was certainly present, but that perhaps they were only half right. I suggested that we try to eliminate the tension myositis pain and see what was left. We embarked on the usual course of treatment, which will be described in detail in a later chapter. The pain began to diminish almost immediately. After about the fourth week he went on a Caribbean vacation with his wife and upon his return told me that during the entire holiday he had been totally free of pain. Upon his return to New York he resumed his usual life and the pain returned, though to a milder degree than before. It was helpful that he had demonstrated to himself that in a situation of complete relaxation his pain could disappear completely. Over the next eight weeks he became progressively free of pain, and about three months from the time of the initial consultation he played tennis for the first time in two years. He has since resumed a completely normal, essentially pain-free existence. Since he is an extremely tense individual he tends to have occasional mild discomfort in the low back but is not inhibited by it in any way.

There is an important postscript to his story. Once having established the diagnosis, the patient and I discussed the fact that he was a very complicated, anxious person. I pointed out that if I were in his shoes I would treat myself to the luxury of psychotherapy. Eventually he accepted the suggestion and apparently has profited from it greatly. While this book was in preparation I received a letter, portions of which are reproduced below.†

---

† "It is just about the first year anniversary of my initial original visit to you and I feel I would be remiss if I did not write and give you a progress report about the condition of my back. I am very happy to report that I am in excellent health and that my back is feeling fine. When friends ask me how I am doing, my constant and uniform response is that my back problems are a thing of the past and that I am doing just great.

"I cannot tell you how great I feel about this, as I have resumed all normal activity, have commenced competitive playing of tennis, both at singles and doubles level, and am enjoying myself thoroughly. I do have some occasional stiffness the day after I play, but almost invariably this is gone by the following morning, and I find even that the resulting stiffness is decreasing in its intensity.

"All in all, I think that my recovery during this past year is quite remarkable, particularly in view of the fact that the only difference in my physical condition is the result of visiting with you, listening to your diagnosis, and trying to put your insights in operation in my daily life."

Although this was a case of severe spondylolisthesis, it is clear that TMS caused the patient's pain. It would be imprecise to say that spondylolisthesis never causes back pain. However, in every case that has come under my care the patient's pain has been due to TMS and not to spondylolisthesis.

I have described a few of the commonest structural abnormalities of the spine to which back pain is routinely attributed. There are many others. Indeed, any deviation in the X-ray appearance of the spine from what is considered "normal" will be blamed for back pain because of the deeply held conviction that the spine is the source of such pain. It is a conviction often without any scientific support.

OTHER "PHYSICAL" DIAGNOSES

Though not actually structural, two other categories of diagnosis are common and must be just as vigorously refuted.

The first of these is inflammation. The frequency with which anti-inflammatory medications are prescribed for back pain reveals the pervasive belief that inflammation somehow contributes to back pain. There is nothing in the medical literature demonstrating that this is so.

What do doctors think is inflamed? Is it the joints of the spine? Is it spinal nerves being compressed by a herniated disc, a bone spur or narrow places in the spinal canal? Doctors seem to hope that anti-inflammatory drugs will counteract whatever is causing inflammation without ever being quite sure what this might be.

An inflammation is an automatic reaction to almost any injury or disease; it is basically a protective, healing process. For example, germs that have gained access to the body will call forth an inflammation whose purpose it is to destroy them. An abscess is the end stage of this kind of inflammatory process, in which the germs have been rounded up, ingested by white blood cells, killed by certain chemicals and sealed off from the rest of the body, creating pus. The symptoms of a cold are largely the result of an inflammatory process. A broken bone will stimulate local inflammation, as will a tear of muscle, ligament or tendon. These reactions are all designed to combat the infection or injury. Some inflammations, however, are the result of strange reactions that are not self-restorative, in which the body turns on itself, so to speak. An example of this is rheumatoid arthritis. In this condition the inflammatory reaction erodes the involved joints. There are other types of inflammation; the subject is too complicated and many-faceted to deal with at length here.

However, there is no demonstrable inflammation in patients with ordinary neck, shoulder or back pain; X rays don't show it; blood tests don't show it. There is no reason to believe that something pressing on a spinal nerve will cause an inflammation, assuming such pressure has occurred. Treating inflammation in back pain is based, therefore, purely on presumption. I have already suggested that TMS is the cause of most back pain and briefly described it. In the succeeding chapters I shall try to make it clear that an alteration in circulation, and not an inflammation, is responsible for most back pain.

Another "physical" diagnosis commonly made is that of strain or sprain. Patients whose pain is restricted to the back, without radiation into either leg or arm, are likely to be told that they are suffering from strain or sprain. Often there is difficulty finding a physical incident to which to attribute these phenomena, but that doesn't deter the diagnostician. Just as often there is something that can be blamed, such as shoveling snow, moving furniture, playing touch football, etc.

The main problem with these diagnoses is that it is difficult to explain patients' reactions on the basis of a strain or a sprain. Patients often describe spasms that come and go over wide areas of the back—something uncharacteristic of sprain or strain. They may even be free of pain for a few hours, only to have it return in a different pattern or place.

Perhaps the most telling clinical point against these diagnoses is that instead of getting better gradually, many patients stay the same or get worse. The body has wonderful recuperative powers. A broken bone will heal in a matter of weeks. One should recover from a strain or a sprain in a few days or, at the most, two or three weeks.

It is hard to escape the conclusion that this is another presumptive diagnosis, made because the diagnostician is unaware of the existence of TMS.

THE IMPORTANCE OF EARLY DIAGNOSIS

It is a truism in medical practice that the earlier a diagnosis is made, the greater the chances for quick, successful treatment. One of the worst aspects of the back pain problem is the tendency to become chronic, brought about first by incorrect diagnoses and second by the fear engendered by those diagnoses. I am convinced that an early diagnosis of TMS will shorten the course of most patients' problems to a matter of days. Much of my time is now spent correcting these misconceptions, dispelling fears, and building confidence, none of which would be necessary with an early, accurate diagnosis.

Let us look at a case history that highlights the consequences of an inaccurate diagnosis.

John was a thirty-five-year-old man who reported a transient episode of low back pain ten years prior to the current episode. He stated that he led a perfectly normal life, including vigorous sports such as tennis after the initial attack. Six weeks before his visit with me he developed sudden severe pain across the entire low back while playing tennis. After a few days the pain spread to include the right buttock, calf and foot, particularly when he stood up. There was also tilting of the trunk when in the upright position. Over the next few weeks he saw three specialists, each of whom suggested that he had a herniated disc and might require hospitalization, a myelogram and possibly surgery. He was advised to remain in bed and take an anti-inflammatory drug and a tranquilizer.

The patient reported that by the end of the third week he was "a wreck"—groggy and nauseated from the medication, physically weak and thoroughly frightened. Finally, realizing that he was making no progress, he found a physician who prescribed a program of physical therapy. He improved somewhat on this regimen but continued to have right buttock and leg pain as well as tilting of the trunk. At this point I saw him in consultation.

On taking his history I learned that he occasionally experienced digestive upsets, had mild hay fever in the spring, suffered occasional attacks of hives and eczema and frequently had a stiff neck. Aside from these minor disorders his health was excellent. Perhaps of the greatest importance, he revealed that he had been under a great deal of strain on his job for a year before the incident on the tennis court.

On physical examination I found a great deal of tenderness when I pressed over muscles in both sides of the neck, the top of both shoulders and the outer aspect of both buttocks, more on the right than the left.

The history and physical examination suggested TMS. Over the next few weeks he participated in my therapeutic program and became pain-free.

This patient's course would have been very different if TMS had been diagnosed when his pain began. The herniated disc diagnosis caused great apprehension, setting in motion the classic vicious cycle. Under the circumstances no conventional treatment would have helped; the bed rest and medication only aggravated the problem by causing additional symptoms.

Now let us look at an alternative scenario. Soon after the onset of pain the patient visits the office of his family physician. After taking the history the doctor examines him and says, "There is nothing to worry about; you have a benign condition brought on by tension involving the muscles of your low back and the right sciatic nerve. In addition to my findings on examination there are two things that point to this diagnosis: Because you are a very conscientious man you have a tendency to develop excess tension, which may express itself physically in stomach symptoms, hay fever, hives, eczema, stiff neck and the tension myositis syndrome. Second, your tough year on the job undoubtedly produced the tension that led to this attack.''

The hypothetical family physician then prescribes a program of gradually increasing exercise and perhaps a short course of physical therapy. He advises the patient that as the pain diminishes he should become increasingly active physically and should eventually return to full activity, including vigorous sports. The physician emphasizes the fact that there is no structural abnormality in the spine, nothing has been injured and there is nothing to fear.

This is how it would be if the existence of TMS were common knowledge. I am suggesting that the diagnosis should be made in the office of the primary physician, either family doctor or internist. It is possible that some patients might not choose to consult a physician at all if they were aware of TMS and confident of its benign nature. Whether or not they went to a doctor, the idea that the process is self-limiting and requires only time for resolution would be reassuring and would set in motion a positive rather than a vicious cycle. Instead of fear and intimidation leading to increasing pain, there would be confidence and rapid improvement.

It is difficult to escape the conclusion that conventional diagnoses unwittingly contribute to the severity and persistence of back pain because they frighten and intimidate.

It might be argued that the therapeutic program prescribed by my hypothetical physician is too simple. To this I would reply that *my* program is more elaborate because I must deal with patients' misconceptions about back pain. I spend a great deal of time telling patients *what they don't have* and allaying their fears. I help them through the process of ''deprogramming''— that is, breaking up the old patterns in which fear leads to more pain. TMS therapy would be much simpler if there were nothing to be undone.

It is interesting to speculate how the world got along without back surgery for so long. I suspect that even though the family physicians of seventy-five years ago were unaware of the existence of TMS, they tended not to take back pain or "sciatica" very seriously. Mustard plasters were widely used and probably brought about relaxation of muscle spasm through the heat generated by the plaster. Sometimes folk medicine is more sensible than "modern" medicine. In any case, I suspect that the low-key, nonthreatening approach to back problems characterized by an earlier time helped to prevent the kind of long-term, disastrous courses that exist today.

Though lacking in the technological medical advances of the latter part of the twentieth century, there often seems to have been a healthier attitude about illness in the "old days." Circumstances required a great deal more dependence upon self-healing, "nature's remedies" and the like. Patients had not been educated to believe that medical treatment could cure all conditions. We need not ignore the magnificent advances that medical science has produced in order to acknowledge that there are untapped sources of healing within us. It is good science to recognize this as well as to continue to search for better drugs and therapeutic techniques. Perhaps a bit more humility is needed in the ranks of medicine.

Chapter 2
Conventional Treatment and Medical Mythology

Conventional treatment for neck and back pain is logical, for it is based upon the conventional diagnostic concept that the pain is due either to a structural abnormality of the spine and associated structures, inflammation, muscle strain or sprain. If one abandons these diagnoses, however, then these treatments lose their rationale. If most neck, shoulder or back pain is due to TMS, very few of the time-honored treatments to be described will be useful.

Perhaps the most universally prescribed treatment, particularly in cases of acute low back and buttock pain, is rest in bed. Patients are usually advised to remain at complete bed rest as long as they can tolerate it, often for weeks at a time. Sometimes the pain disappears with bed rest; in many cases it remains unchanged or gets worse. It is not difficult to imagine that the symptoms of patients with TMS, forced to neglect their responsibilities, might get worse. The mother with a young child or someone who is self-employed can become extremely apprehensive as the days go by, thereby increasing what is causing the pain—tension. If bed rest comforts the patient, the outcome will be favorable; if it increases anxiety, it is counterproductive.

To enforce strict bed rest, particularly if the patient is in the hospital, traction is often ordered. Most commonly, a fifteen-pound weight with a pulley arrangement is attached to a harness encircling the lower part of the trunk. This small amount of weight exerts an insignificant pull on the lower part of the spine, but it serves to keep the patient in bed.

Neck traction (cervical) is often used for patients with neck or shoulder pain, particularly those diagnosed as having a "pinched nerve." Here the purpose is to separate the bones of the neck, even if only a millimeter or two, and larger amounts of weights are used. With a harness attached to the head, there are machines designed to exert just the right amount of pull, often intermittently. Cervical traction is not needed if the pain is due to TMS.

The use of neck collars and body corsets is based upon the principles of immobilization and "support." The latter is a nebulous concept here, for it is hard to see how the devices used for neck or back pain can give such support. Neither do they immobilize. But in any case, there is no reason to use them if TMS is responsible for the pain, for one wants movement, not immobilization. The patients I see in consultation have not benefited from conventional treatment and so usually report that collars and corsets are not helpful. However, there must be many patients who find them useful. If they have TMS it is likely that a successful result can be attributed to psychological rather than physical factors. This may be said of any treatment; that phenomenon is known as the *placebo* effect. (The word placebo is Latin, meaning "I will please.")

Originally placebo referred to any inactive substance given in the form of medication to please or gratify the patient. Later, when it was realized that placebos could actually make patients feel better or even cure a disorder, the placebo effect came to be recognized as a legitimate and important reaction, though no one could explain it. It then became common medical practice to test the effectiveness of a new drug by comparing it to a placebo. The method generally employed is to give half of a large group of patients the new drug and the other half a placebo— that is, a pill that looks the same as the real medication but is composed of an inactive substance. If the new drug is effective—that is, if it does what it's supposed to do—the group of patients receiving the real medication should respond better than those receiving the placebo. If the placebo performs as well or almost as well as the drug being tested, it indicates that the new drug is no better than an inert substance. What is of great interest is that the placebo is capable of doing anything at all. The significance of this phenomenon is enormous, but it has not yet been fully developed by medical science.

What is the placebo reaction? All forms of treatment, such as manipulations, exercise or acupuncture, can act physically or they can act as a placebo. The essence of a placebo reaction is that the person receiving the treatment subconsciously *believes* it has value, that it's going to be effective. In that case, any treatment can relieve pain. Pain is a symptom, not a disease process. It is a signal that something is wrong; it may be a broken bone, a stomach ulcer, an infection or TMS. In each case there is a physiologic reaction that results in pain. A placebo can reduce the pain in each of these examples by either or both of two mechanisms:

1. A placebo can reduce the tension temporarily by creating a belief in the patient's mind that he or she is going to be cured, as in the case of ulcers or TMS.
2. A placebo can reduce or abolish any kind of pain temporarily by stimulating the secretion of certain chemicals in the brain known as endorphins, as in the case of TMS or a broken bone. These chemicals are the brain's own ''pain-killers,'' and they are much more effective than any produced outside the body.

In either case, *belief* produces the result, suggesting that psychological factors govern placebo reactions.

Patients with TMS often report having been completely relieved of symptoms for weeks or months after surgery. I believe this occurs sometimes because surgery is a powerful placebo, perhaps the ultimate placebo. The effectiveness of a placebo is directly proportional to the impression it makes on the patient's subconscious mind. It is a formidable decision to undergo surgery; subconsciously the patient says, "This must make me better."

In my experience the pain in these cases inevitably recurred, suggesting another rule: The placebo effect is almost always *temporary*. Furthermore, since the treatment did nothing to alleviate the underlying cause of the pain, it usually returns *in exactly the same pattern*. In general, types of treatment less dramatic than surgery, as in those employing manipulation or acupuncture, give relief for shorter periods of time, usually a matter of days, thus necessitating an ongoing program of treatment. In some cases the treatments eventually lose their effectiveness and patients become disillusioned. It is not known why the placebo effect is temporary; it is simply an observed fact.

The placebo reaction is a logical explanation for the treatment history of my patients with TMS before they learned the correct diagnosis. Indeed, it is now clear to me why some of my patients with back pain improved and others did not in the years before I began to make the TMS diagnosis. Those who had confidence in me and/or the physical therapy treatment I prescribed got better; the others did not.

I believe the placebo reaction continues to be a factor with some of the patients I treat currently. Some find it difficult to accept the diagnosis of TMS, for a variety of reasons. Usually they are willing to accept the idea that there is no structural problem, but they have trouble attributing the pain to tension. These patients invest their confidence in the physical therapy program, particularly the exercises. They have a good, sometimes prolonged, placebo response but invariably have a recurrence of pain. Very often I am consulted when this happens and the patient reveals that there has been some new source of tension. The unconscious tendency to resist the diagnosis continues, nevertheless, meaning that the placebo effect will determine whether the pain will recur.

In recent years many respected medical investigators have recognized that placebos can induce striking reactions in the body. Their observations have revealed that placebos can produce a positive effect in a wide range of physical and mental disorders, including drug addiction, arthritis, hypertension, peptic ulcers, hay fever and many others.

There has also been discussion in medical circles as to whether it is ethical knowingly to use placebos to treat patients, since one is "fooling the patient." In my view, the question reflects a limited understanding of how placebos work and what they mean. A placebo "cure" is temporary and therefore of limited value; eventually it no longer works. Therefore, why would a doctor knowingly use it as a treatment? More to the point is the question of why placebos work and for which medical conditions and patients.

The placebo effect depends on subconscious *belief* and, therefore, may be particularly effective in disorders that originate in the mind, more specifically in the unconscious, emotional part of the mind. That includes TMS, peptic ulcer, colitis and many other conditions.

Let us now return to the description of conventional treatment techniques.

Closely allied to bed rest and immobilization is the principle of restricting physical activity. Patients are advised to do as little as possible and particularly to avoid exerting themselves. During the acute phase of an episode of pain such instructions are unnecessary, but as patients improve or if the pain becomes chronic, this is a routine prescription.

In virtually every case medications are prescribed, the most common being "muscle relaxants," tranquilizers, anti-inflammatory drugs and "pain-killers." Because muscle spasm is so common, use of the first two categories of medications is very logical. Again, because I may see only the failures of conventional treatment, they are rarely successful in my experience. Like tranquilizers, "muscle relaxants" do not work directly on the muscle but exert whatever effect they may have in the brain.

Anti-inflammatory medications taken by mouth include a wide variety of substances, ranging from aspirin to cortisone-type drugs (steroids). As stated previously, since there is no evidence for the existence of inflammation in these pain syndromes, the occasional success of these drugs must be based upon the placebo effect. They are not prescribed in the routine treatment of TMS.

Pain-killers are always indicated when pain is severe; often the use of narcotics is justified. However, no one employs these drugs except as a temporary expedient.

A number of medicinal substances are administered by injection. Steroids are sometimes injected into painful muscles or around the spine. More commonly, a local anesthetic agent, such as procaine, is injected into the center of a painful area in the neck, shoulders or back. Sometimes called "trigger-point injections," they can produce dramatic relief from acute pain. Since I have concluded that most pain in these areas is due to TMS, I rarely employ this technique, having found that it is temporary and does not contribute to the basic solution of the problem. On occasion I use it in someone with acute, severe pain.

Another injection technique, widely used by specialists in anesthesiology, is to block with a local anesthetic nerves that are thought to be transmitting pain signals to the brain. This is reasonable regardless of the cause of the pain but, once more, it does not solve the underlying problem. It is probably used often because of the unspoken conviction that there is some structural problem causing the pain, such as arthritis, that won't go away, and so one might as well try to block the pain. If successful, however, this kind of treatment must be repeated indefinitely. Since the goal of treatment for TMS is to eliminate the pain permanently and completely, nerve blocks are never employed.

It is probably not well known among laymen, but the principle behind acupuncture is to block the transmission of pain signals from the painful part of the body to the brain, just as a nerve block does. Pain is not pain until it is registered as such in the brain. Local anesthetics—as used by a dentist, for example—prevent the pain signal from getting to the brain by interfering with the normal function of nerves in the gums. In a manner that remains mysterious to this day, acupuncture appears to block the transmission of pain signals. There is some evidence that it does this in the spinal cord and also somewhere in the brain itself.

Based on how acupuncture works, the same objection applies to its use for patients with neck, shoulder or back pain as the objection to muscle or nerve blocks with a local anesthetic. This is no doubt the reason why patients I have seen reported that acupuncture helped temporarily or not at all.

Another widely used technique for blocking the transmission of painful signals is transcutaneous nerve stimulation (TNS). Skin electrodes are placed over painful areas of the back, for example, and mild electric shocks are produced by a small device worn by the patient. The shocks are supposed to stimulate the nerves in the region and block the pain signal. However, a study done at the Mayo Clinic and reported by Dr. G. Thorsteinsson and three colleagues[1] showed that almost as many people were helped by a placebo nerve stimulator as by the real one, suggesting that many patients treated with TNS feel less pain because they want to or think they are supposed to. TNS is used primarily for patients with severe, chronic, disabling back pain.

Biofeedback is a new treatment method occasionally used for these pain syndromes. The technique most frequently employed attempts to produce total body relaxation by placing electrodes over certain muscles, usually at the forehead, so that the muscular activity is registered on a machine and is seen and heard by the patient. The principle of this technique is that the patient will learn to reduce activity in the forehead muscle and in so doing bring about reflex relaxation all over the body. It is a good idea but does not solve the problem of TMS because it treats the symptom, pain, and not the underlying cause.

Another widely used treatment for neck, shoulder and back pain is exercise. It has had some staunch proponents, both inside and outside of medicine, despite the fact that the rationale for its use is very unclear. The most common reason given is that exercise strengthens the muscles of the abdomen and back and that this somehow eliminates the pain. As described earlier, conventional diagnoses most often attribute the pain to some structural abnormality. If the pain is due to protruding disc material or an arthritic bone spur, for example, what possible purpose would be served by strengthening muscles? If the pain is due to a strain or sprain of back muscles, the best treatment would be to rest the involved muscles for a few days.

What of the proposition that the pain is due to weak muscles? That idea is very hard to reconcile with the facts that there are millions of sedentary people of both sexes and all ages who don't have back pain and that a fair proportion of the patients I have treated through the years have been healthy, strong young men and women.

On the other hand, as I point out in Chapter 5, "The Treatment of TMS," there is a place for exercise when TMS is the cause of pain, since exercise may improve the blood circulation to the involved muscles and nerves.

In my experience, the value of exercise in eliminating or preventing back pain for conventional diagnoses must be attributed to its strong placebo effect. Conversations with patients make it very clear that exercises are often performed with almost religious, ritualistic regularity in the belief that this will ward off the pain. This is the essence of the placebo reaction.

Among other conventional treatments, manipulation techniques are widely used, primarily by nonphysicians. They are based on the principle that misalignments of the spine are responsible for neck, shoulder or back pain. Some practitioners believe that such misalignments are responsible for many other conditions as well. The treatment is designed to restore proper alignment by manipulation. The trouble with this approach is that there is no evidence that the misalignments to which the pain is attributed are abnormal or cause pain. They are seen on X ray, but as reported in Chapter 1, Dr. Splithoff found no difference in the incidence of nine different abnormalities of the lower spine as seen on X ray in patients with and without back pain. Even such time-honored abnormalities as herniated disc appear not to cause pain in most cases. The minor misalignments for which manipulation is employed are hardly likely to cause pain.

To what, then, does one attribute the occasional success of this method? Patient responses again suggest the placebo effect. Because the placebo effect is temporary, these patients must return for treatment regularly. Some continue for many years; others do well for a while and then no longer derive benefit from treatments. Most patients I have spoken with do not get total relief from pain and remain very restricted in physical activity.

We come finally to what is without doubt the most formidable treatment for back pain—surgery. There are many conditions for which spine surgery is prescribed, including the removal of tumors and the correction of abnormalities caused by a violent injury to the spine when there is clear evidence of fracture or dislocation. There are also cases in which there has been a large herniation of disc material that produces obvious neurological changes—partial or complete paralysis of the legs, for example, and bowel and bladder dysfunction. There is no question concerning the necessity for surgery in these cases. The problem arises with respect to many people with low back and leg pain whose CT scans or myelograms (see page 17) show disc abnormalities but whose pain is coming from TMS. I first treated such patients because they had decided not to have surgery and sought nonsurgical treatment. I was surprised to find that treating for TMS eliminated the pain completely, suggesting that no part of the pain was due to the herniated disc. It has been many years since the first patient was so treated, and since then I have seen very few patients whose herniated discs were the cause of the pain. An overwhelming majority have been treated successfully.

Surgery to stabilize the spine, a spinal fusion, was once commonly performed but now has lost favor with many doctors who used to do the procedure.

The enzyme papain has been used for many years in Canada and more recently in the United States to dissolve disc material. This is a nonsurgical method for removing disc material thought to be causing nerve pain by compression. The practice is logical if that is the cause of the pain. Since TMS is the cause of most back pain, one can only conclude that "cures" are due to the placebo effect, as they appear to be with surgery.

Again, because these treatments are temporary, we must conclude that their success is the result of the placebo effect. If we follow the course of surgically treated patients long enough, we find that the majority develop pain again, often in a similar pattern to that which they had prior to surgery. Many patients will develop other tension-related disorders: tension headaches, acid indigestion or ulcers, colitis, etc. This pattern is common when a physical condition caused by tension is eliminated by a placebo treatment.

In summary, conventional treatments of neck, shoulder and back pain often fail because they are based on inaccurate diagnoses. When they succeed, only temporarily, success must be attributed to the placebo effect.

MEDICAL MYTHOLOGY

Over the years many theories have developed to explain back pain and how to prevent it. Most of these have been fostered by medical concepts of causation, but since they are based on unproven assumptions they fall into the categories of folklore or mythology.

The Disc Myth

One of the basic myths, fundamental to many others, is that the back is a delicate structure, to be protected carefully from strain or damage. The public is advised never to pick up things unless the knees are bent and the back straight in order to minimize pressure within the lumbar intervertebral discs. Dr. Alf Nachemson, an orthopedic surgeon from Gothenburg, Sweden, has indeed demonstrated that high pressures are generated within these discs when the trunk is inclined forward, and they are higher still if one lifts something at the same time.[2] But there is no proof that this is bad for the back or hastens degeneration of the discs. Dr. Nachemson has pointed out that discs normally begin to degenerate in the early twenties. I fail to see that this is any more pathological than any other part of the aging process. But the mythology of the lumbar disc is pervasive. Patients are bombarded by both practitioners and the media with information about how spinal discs degenerate, deteriorate, protrude and herniate. It seems so simple: If these things happen, they must cause pain. It was also very simple and apparent even to brilliant minds a few hundred years ago that the earth was the center of the universe. The reason for this obsession with discs is that it does seem logical. There are those degenerating structures at the lower end of the spine, right where a lot of pain and spasms occur; there are lumbar and sacral nerves conveniently located so that they can be compressed by bulging or herniated discs; there is pain in the leg, proving that those nerves are compressed.

It is very neat but in many cases it is wrong—a myth created and perpetuated by the medical profession and the media. The question is not whether discs degenerate and herniate; they do. What is at issue is whether disc abnormalities cause pain.

The disc myth is particularly dangerous because it often leads to surgery. With the recent advent of the CT scan X-ray technique, more and more herniated discs are being identified, and thus more surgery is advised and undertaken.

The Ape Myth

The idea of the vulnerability of the back was greatly enhanced a number of years ago when a doctor suggested that the problem of back pain was due to the fact that man was not meant to walk upright. Here is mankind's imagination at its most fertile. We have become so attached to the belief that back pain is the result of structural abnormalities of the spine that we are willing to foist a totally illogical idea onto the process of evolution. Darwin would have been shocked.

It is my understanding that the process of evolution is characterized by two fundamental principles: (1) There is a powerful tendency for all species to perpetuate themselves, and (2) in order to accomplish this, each species will adapt in a variety of ways, even to the point of changing its basic structures and systems. Adaptation and change are in the service of perpetuation, or to use a term more commonly employed, the survival of species. Species that adapt successfully survive; others, such as the dinosaurs, do not.

Homo sapiens has evolved to be the dominant animal on this planet. To be sure, his brain has a great deal to do with this dominance, but it took millions of years for the brain to develop, and during that time our ancestors had to survive physically. They could not have done so if the spine was maladapted for the upright posture.

In 1974 Dr. Donald Johanson unearthed the remains of a hominid ancestor of man in Africa; he called this ancestor *Australopithecus afarensis*. An unusually large number of bones were found, permitting a detailed reconstruction of the skeletal anatomy of this individual. Students of anthropology have been surprised by the fact that this ancestor of ours walked upright. *A. afarensis* lived about three and a half million years ago. This discovery makes even more ludicrous the modern medical belief that humans were not meant to walk on their hind legs.

From a purely mechanical point of view, the upright posture should be easier on the spine than walking on all fours. Look at swaybacked horses. It is well known in veterinary medicine that dachshunds are quite prone to catastrophic disc herniation with paralysis of the hind legs. This is unusual in human beings.

Nonsense explanations for back pain are inevitable in view of medicine's failure to recognize the pathophysiology of back pain. The spine is perfectly sound; the culprit is excessive tension in an age of anxiety.

Common Prohibitions and Admonitions
"Sit up straight."

Variations: "Sit in a straight chair that supports the contour of your back." "Don't slouch." "Sitting in a soft chair or on a couch leaves your spine unsupported and causes pain."

These ideas are unsupported by objective evidence, but they seem logical to most patients because pain aggravated or brought on by sitting is a common complaint. This is due to the fact that the individual often sits on a sore muscle and because once one associates pain with sitting, it becomes a self-fulfilling prophecy.

"Don't sit with your legs crossed."

I don't understand this one. In my experience it has no relevance to the problem. There are literally dozens of maneuvers, postures, positions, etc., that can be associated with pain. Most of these associations are the result of conditioning; one comes to expect pain under certain conditions, and so it happens.

"Don't stand still."

Or: "Don't stand still; if you must, try to put one foot up on a stool (or bar rail). This takes some of the curve out of your low back; the curve is bad because it produces pressure on spinal nerves."

Many patients complain that standing in one place causes or aggravates low back pain. This is not, however, because of "pressure on spinal nerves." It probably results from the fact that the inactivity promotes slowed circulation in the low back and buttock muscles. These patients feel better when they move around. When TMS comes under control, this ceases to be a problem.

"Sleep on a hard mattress."

One of the most deeply rooted, pervasive myths is the idea that a hard sleeping surface is good for your back. I can imagine how this myth began. I picture a man talking to his doctor about the terrible back pain he awakened with one morning. The doctor asks what he thinks is a logical question:

"What kind of a bed do you have?"

"Well, now that you mention it, it's a very old bed, the springs are sagging, and it has a soft, lumpy mattress."

"Aha! That's the answer. Your back has been unsupported and crooked because of that bed. No wonder you have back pain."

If one's concept of the cause of back pain is centered on the spine, the doctor's conclusion is logical. There is no evidence to support this. This myth is so deeply ingrained in people's minds that it forms the basis for a business of considerable magnitude. Everyone accepts it as gospel that a hard mattress is good for one's back. The idea has taken hold so firmly that a whole generation of people will never experience the joys of a soft, enveloping mattress.

Patients often say, "But I like sleeping on a hard mattress." That is another matter entirely. If you prefer a hard mattress, that's fine. There is certainly nothing wrong with it.

With the expectation that a hard surface will be beneficial, the individual with back pain often experiences relief by lying on a hard mattress, or the floor. Conversely, the expectation that a soft mattress will cause pain invariably brings on the pain. This is hard to accept for many patients. They often say, "How do you know that this is due to conditioning?" My evidence is the long-term success of our therapeutic approach. Having recovered from TMS, my patients can lie on a soft couch with pleasure.

"High heels are bad for your back."

This probably derives from the fact that wearing high heels tends to increase the lumbar (lordotic) curve, and it is claimed that anything which does that can cause back pain by narrowing the openings through which the spinal nerves pass. This is an idea, to be sure, but it is totally unsupported by objective evidence. The next one is quite similar.

"Don't swim the crawl or the breast stroke."

This admonition is designed to prevent arching the low back, which is thought to produce back pain by compression of the spinal nerves. This, too, is an unproven theory. Many of my patients have helped to disprove it by ignoring it at my suggestion.

"Don't lie on your back or stomach."

This, too, has to do with the arch in the lumbar spine; nothing need be added to the previous paragraphs.

"Being overweight is bad for your back."

My impression is that the excess weight is supposed to put an increased load on the spine, or the weight of a protruding abdomen increases the lumbar arch. In either case there is no evidence that overweight increases or causes back pain.

"Flat feet cause backache."

There is no evidence that this is so.

"Put a lift in your shoe."

One of the oldest ideas around is that discrepancies in the length of the legs cause back pain. It is very common for one leg to be shorter than the other by as much as one-half inch. Though this is perfectly normal, it has been claimed that it causes a tilt in the pelvis and that this produces back pain. This is an-other unfounded assertion, a cherished myth.

"Don't run if you have back pain."

As running has increased in popularity in recent years, it was inevitable that there would be a proliferation of experts on the problems experienced by runners. Of course, many bona fide injuries may occur when runners overextend themselves or sim-ply have unavoidable accidents. But there are a number of mis-conceptions about the effects on the back of running that do not bear the stamp of objective validation.

One of the most basic of these is the idea that the pounding experienced by the runner is bad for the spine. As usual, the idea seems logical, especially when there is evidence that the lumbar intervertebral discs degenerate as we get older so that we lose the shock-absorbing function of these structures. In my ex-perience, however, this is not pathological, and the spine ad-justs to the changing structure of the discs. All biological systems have a great capacity for adaptation.

Over the years I have treated many men and women who were advised to stop running or playing any active sport because of a history of low back pain. A large proportion of these were diagnosed as having disc disease and were warned that such vig-orous physical activity would lead to further deterioration and possible dire results. Whether or not this was explicitly stated, the specter of loss of leg strength was always in the patient's mind.

When it was apparent that these men and women were actually suffering from TMS, they were routinely encouraged to resume the forbidden activities as soon as they had completed the appropriate treatment program. I cannot recall a single case of a patient who successfully completed my program and was unable to resume vigorous athletic activity. This was sometimes difficult to do, since apprehension based upon the person's previous experience was great and often took time to eliminate. Fear is often buried in the unconscious and may take a while to eradicate, but as the individual recognizes that the source of the pain is TMS and regains confidence in the back, the outcome is uniformly good.

I remember a young man who first developed back pain while playing tennis. He went through the treatment program successfully and was soon back on the tennis court. About two years later I received a telephone call from him during which he said he was doing fine, playing tennis regularly, but wanted to know why he occasionally had a little back discomfort after he finished playing—"not always, but once or twice a month." I reminded him that since his first attack of back pain occurred while playing tennis there must have been a small residue of apprehension about tennis in his unconscious mind, which occasionally caused mild back pain. Fear is often impossible to eradicate completely.

Patients sometimes report that their pain starts while running or jogging, though it may begin hours or days after a run. The presence of TMS makes this perfectly logical and allows one to encourage these patients to resume running when the pain is gone. Running, like swimming, is one of the best cardiovascular conditioners and ways of burning off tension. This is the great tragedy of prohibiting these vigorous activities; the individual loses an important means of dissipating accumulated tension while apprehension about his back compounds the tension.

A number of "injuries" of the legs and feet are associated

with running. Some of these, such as hamstring or calf tears, stress fractures and shin splints, are real. However, in my practice I have found that painful conditions in the legs or feet are often the result of tendinitis, or lumbar spinal or sciatic nerve irritation. The most common leg tendinitis I have encountered is around the knee, involving the ligaments on either side of the joint. Less frequently, the patellar (kneecap) or Achilles tendons may be involved. These are associated with TMS, and successful treatment of TMS often leads to the disappearance of tendinitis. This might take longer to go away than muscle and nerve pain.

I have been an early-morning runner for nineteen years, averaging between ten and twenty miles a week all year round. I have experienced a variety of back, leg and foot pains through the years but have never had to stop running, since they all appeared to be manifestations of TMS. I am certain I would have stopped many times had I been unaware of the existence of TMS.

A recent experience is a good example. I was about a half mile into a three-mile run when I began to feel pain in the left calf. I stopped, satisfied myself that there was no local process at work, such as phlebitis or an inflammation, and concluded that the pain was due to TMS sciatica.

Having concluded that it was TMS, I decided to continue the run. I did so, and by the time I got home, the pain was gone. The same thing happened on two succeeding mornings, with diminishing intensity. On the fourth morning there was no pain. Had I attributed the sciatica to a disc problem I am sure the outcome would have been vastly different.

I have devoted the first two chapters of this book to a description of conventional diagnoses and treatment in order to answer in advance questions that might arise in the course of the description of TMS and its treatment. It is hard to abandon concepts one has taken for granted for a long time, but progress requires it. Neck, shoulder and back pain are recognized everywhere as an unsolved problem of major proportions. In the remaining chapters I shall describe the diagnosis and treatment of TMS in the hope that it will enlighten both doctors and the victims of back pain.

Chapter 3
What Causes Back Pain? The Psychophysiology of TMS

Neck, shoulder and back pain is not a mechanical problem to be cured by mechanical means. It has to do with people's feelings, their personalities and the vicissitudes of life. Above all, back pain is a reflection of temperament, which is undoubtedly why back pain is so common. Americans are a nation of doers and workers. We take life seriously and responsibly. As our lives become more complex, we generate more and more tension. This is the basis for most back pain.

The key word in tension production is personality. There is a distinct TMS personality, though it is not unique to TMS patients. It is shared by people who experience analagous physical disorders, such as ulcers or colitis. Indeed, the TMS personality is similar in some respects to that of so-called type A individuals, who have been identified as prone to coronary disease by Drs. M. Friedman and R. H. Rosenman in their book *Type A Behavior and Your Heart.*[1] The difference seems to be a matter of degree; type A people are extremely compulsive about their work and responsibilities; they leave no time for play or relaxation and accept no limits on their need to achieve. Although TMS people are conscientious, responsible, hardworking and often compulsive, they usually are aware of their limitations and the need to take time out. They seem to be in better touch with themselves emotionally. In both groups, however, the drive comes primarily from within; life circumstances only add fuel to the fire of their need to accomplish, or live up to some ideal role, such as being the best parent, student or worker.

A typical example was a patient who through compulsive hard work established a very successful business and became the patriarch and benefactor of his large family. He enjoyed the role but felt the responsibility deeply. Throughout his entire adult life he experienced low back pain, which resisted all attempts at treatment. By the time I saw him the pain patterns were deeply ingrained and part of his everyday life. He understood the concept of tension-induced pain but was unable to erase the patterns of a lifetime. The primary benefit he derived from treatment was the reassurance that there was nothing structurally wrong with his back.

Another patient was a young man in his twenties who had his first child two months before he opened a new branch of the family hardware business. The simultaneous imposition of these new responsibilities in this very conscientious young man induced TMS of the low back. As soon as he became aware of the source of the pain—tension—it promptly disappeared. This occurs frequently with TMS patients; why and how it happens will be discussed in Chapter 5, "The Treatment of TMS."

What these two patients had in common was a great sense of responsibility and a strong inner drive to succeed in both business and family matters. Such people do not need to be monitored; they are self-motivated, self-disciplined, their own severest critics. This is one of the most common sources of tension.

Though personality is primary, life circumstances also play a role in producing tension. I recall a high school teacher who pumped gas at a local filling station on Saturdays to augment his income. One Saturday I received an emergency call that he was having severe chest pain. On examination there was no evidence of a cardiac problem, and his cardiogram was normal; the pain was clearly muscular in origin. When it was all over and I was able to talk to him we concluded that the humiliation of working at the gas station, where some of his students could see him, had produced a great deal of tension, with the result described. We agreed that he might better find some other way of adding to his income.

Although work-related tension is common and easily recognized, family dynamics often produce serious problems that may be unrecognized because of their subtlety. One of my patients was a woman of Mediterranean origin in her late forties. She had a sheltered adolescence, married early and, as demanded by her culture, thereafter devoted herself exclusively to home and family. She did an excellent job since she was an intelligent, competent and compassionate woman. However, there came a time when she began to resent the facts that she had not been allowed to go to school as a child and could not read and write, that her family discouraged her desire to learn to drive a car and that their needs so thoroughly dominated her life. As she was not truly conscious of this resentment, it manifested itself in a long, disabling history of back pain, including unsuccessful surgery. When her case came to my attention she was in constant pain and was almost totally unable to function. In the course of treatment as she learned about her repressed feelings and determined to make changes in her life, the pain seemed to melt away. The process was not without psychological trauma, for she was faced with the disapproval of family and friends as well as her own deeply etched attitudes. What she then experienced was psychological pain, which was appropriate to the situation, and not an inappropriate substitute, back pain. It was worth it, she said, to be liberated from the physical pain.

The combination of certain personality traits and life situations often produces psychological conflicts, a common source of tension. I remember a woman I had successfully treated for low back pain about two years before who called one day to tell me that she had now developed neck, shoulder and arm pain but was quite sure it was due to a painful psychological situation involving her husband and teenage stepdaughter. I encouraged her to carry on without seeking treatment. Over the next few months the psychological situation remained unresolved, the pain was severe and eventually she lost a good bit of motion in both shoulders, despite which she resisted all advice to have new diagnostic tests and treatment. Then one day she decided to face the problem squarely and confront her husband. The result was a surprisingly easy solution that defused the entire situation; with it, she said, the pain ceased. She began to exercise systematically and gradually recovered all of the lost movement in her shoulders.The correlation between psychological conflict and physical pain is clearly evident in this case history. Unresolved conflict produces tension, and tension can find an outlet in pain.

Sometimes the source of the tension is not obvious. I recall a young married woman who reacted to the diagnosis of TMS with great surprise. She denied being tense or nervous and said that she was not particularly conscientious or compulsive. The friend who accompanied her confirmed this and said she was known to be a very jolly, easygoing person. Only after a long discussion did she reveal that her strategy for coping with life's problems was to put them out of her mind. She said she simply would not allow anything to bother her.

This is a foolproof formula for generating tension. Putting things out of one's mind doesn't get rid of them; it simply relegates them to the unconscious, where they are free to create anxiety quite undisturbed. This hidden tension then manifests itself in a physical disorder, such as TMS.

What is tension? Where does it come from? I have suggested that it is the result of certain personality traits and life situations, but if we look a bit more deeply it would appear that there are other factors underlying the need to be responsible or achieving or strong. To some extent we all strive to prove that we are worthwhile, or that we are good, or strong. Doesn't everyone want to be loved, approved of, admired? These are basic needs, but usually they are below the level of consciousness and, what is more important, they are often in conflict with other unconscious drives. Often the man who acts strong or tough has underlying feelings of vulnerability or the desire to be taken care of, which he feels he must suppress because they are not "manly." The resultant "battle," which rages unknown to him, is the source of tension. People who push themselves on the job may resent the necessity of working so hard, of being under constant pressure. On the other hand, how can you prove that you're a worthwhile person if you're not a success?

Although the need to be loved and approved of is virtually universal, the things one may have to do to win approval are often in conflict with other needs. The woman of Mediterranean origin I described earlier wanted to be a good mother, but she also wanted some things for herself. The result: repressed anger and feelings of guilt. The sequence: conflict leading to tension, tension causing back pain.

Tension is not always negative. A certain amount of it is necessary for normal functioning; it provides a kind of energy for our daily activities. When the amount of tension exceeds our daily needs, trouble begins.

The well-known psychoanalyst, Karen Horney, has written about the "tyranny of the should."[2] "I should be a good worker (good parent, good provider, thoughtful son or daughter, good citizen)." This is where tension often comes from: the battle that goes on in the subconscious part of the mind between the "shoulds" and the "don't give a damns."

One of the worst aspects of TMS is that the process seems to be self-generating. Once it begins, a vicious cycle usually develops in which a variety of factors tend to add to the person's anxiety, thereby increasing the pain. For example, pain itself is anxiety-producing and so causes more pain.

Confusion about the diagnosis is another source of anxiety. Most back pain sufferers have been to a variety of physicians and other types of practitioners and have been given many different explanations for the pain. In time they become thoroughly confused and very fearful about what may be going on in their backs.

Many of the terms, such as "degeneration" and "deterioration," are frightening. The patient imagines the lower end of the spine eventually crumbling, paralysis of the legs, a wheelchair, permanent disability. These are fearsome things to contemplate and they terrorize patients, increasing anxiety and pain.

I recall a woman who said she left her doctor's office in a state of shock and almost fainted as she walked down the street after being told that the lower end of her spine was degenerating. Another woman patient said that she decided to seek advice on how to eliminate a very mild problem. She found that occasionally after she played a game of tennis there was some discomfort in her low back, and she thought she'd like to discover the reason. X rays were taken, and she was told that the L5-S1 disc was deteriorated and was the reason for the discomfort. It was suggested that she stop playing tennis and in general be careful of all physical activity. Until that time she had been leading a perfectly normal life. Over the next few months her pain gradually increased in severity, and in addition she began to have pain in the left leg. With each passing week she became less active and more frightened. By the time I saw her she had a full-blown pain syndrome, including occasional attacks of severe spasm, which kept her in bed for two or three days at a time. She was convinced that the degenerative process in the lower end of her spine was progressing, that now there was nerve compression causing leg pain and that she would probably have to undergo surgery.

It is quite clear that the doctor's diagnosis was the reason for the escalation of her pain. On examination she had typical manifestations of TMS, and when reassured that the X-ray abnormalities were benign and quite normal for someone her age, she began to improve promptly. In a couple of months she was back to her normal routine, including tennis.

Another great fear that serves to intensify and perpetuate TMS is that of physical activity. An acute attack invariably brings forth the prescription of bed rest. This is based on the concept that a structural abnormnality must be allowed to heal or an inflammatory process must be resolved. Sometimes the pain will improve on such a regimen; often it does not, but the patient can't tolerate remaining in bed and begins to move around.

However, all activity is undertaken with great trepidation. "You must not bend, lift things or exert yourself in any way" is a common warning issued by both physicians and laymen. Little by little the patient becomes conditioned, programmed; even the thought of physical activity can arouse apprehension. The result is an increase in TMS and more pain. Again, it's a vicious cycle.

But still another set of psychological factors add to the reservoir of anxiety. Invariably the person begins to feel very inadequate. A mother with young children finds she can't lift them or play with them as she did before. A father can't play with his boy, throw a football or ski with him. The homemaker isn't able to vacuum or bend over to make the beds; standing at the sink is agonizing—the slight forward bend makes the back hurt even more. Social activities have to be curtailed—one can't sit at a movie, can't have company or go bowling. All of these things are either prohibited by pain or bring it on.

Sexual activity often aggravates back pain, though this point is rarely discussed. Lovemaking is a very physical activity, and either partner may be unable to function normally because of the fear or reality of increased pain.

Invariably the breadwinner begins to worry about losing time from work, job security, financial loss and the specter of possibly not being able to work at all. It is easy to see how people begin to feel desperate and why the anxiety and pain escalate. They often become irritable and depressed to the point of hopelessness, no longer responding to treatments or medications that were previously helpful.

What is the destination of this excess tension? As it does not evaporate it must be dissipated, used up or burned up. One might postulate a law of the conservation of psychic energy—that once generated, energies such as tension must be expressed in some way. The most logical and direct way for tension to manifest itself should be in the emotions, for that's where it originates. But that would mean that the person would feel jittery, nervous or uptight. These are unpleasant feelings, and they are unacceptable to the person who has them and to the outside world. We don't like to feel out of control, and don't like to be known as jittery, nervous individuals. Because the emotional manifestations of excess tension are individually and socially unacceptable, the brain chooses to channel the tension elsewhere—namely, the body. I shall describe how this is accomplished physically in a moment, but first we should try to understand the rationale for this strategy of sublimation a little better.

Trouble in the mind or with the emotions is still not socially acceptable. Although people are gradually becoming more enlightened about such things, most still have a strong aversion to admitting to emotional difficulties or, worse, seeking help from a psychiatrist or psychologist. Many doctors reinforce these attitudes. They prefer to treat physical disorders; they feel insecure when faced with emotional problems and often have no patience with them. Their usual response is to prescribe a medication and hope that the problem will go away. People are sensitive to these attitudes.

On the other hand, people with physical illnesses rarely face these prejudices. Medical insurance will pay for the most elaborate of physical treatments, including thousands of dollars for diagnostic studies and expensive surgery, but most policies exclude or sharply limit payment for psychotherapy.

In light of this, the mind develops a strategy designed to avoid the appearance of emotional difficulty. Quite unconsciously, the tension is channeled into the body, and a physical disorder is made to *substitute* for the emotional manifestation of tension. Now the patient need feel no shame; the tension is *hidden*.

This is very common, and I doubt that there is anyone who has not experienced or will not experience one or more of these physical substitutes during their lifetime. Such physical reactions are called *psychophysiologic* disorders—that is, physical changes caused by some emotional phenomenon. They include TMS; a variety of stomach ailments, including heartburn, "nervous stomach," gastritis, ulcer and hiatus hernia; colitis; spastic colon; tension headache; migraine headache; hives; eczema; hay fever and asthma, to name the most common.

A number of years ago, when I was beginning to suspect that tension was responsible for most back pain, I did a survey of a large group of patients with TMS and found that 88 percent had a history of one or more of these conditions; 28 percent had experienced *four* or more during their lives.

I must acknowledge a debt of gratitude to columnist Russell Baker, who asked in one of his Sunday columns in *The New York Times Magazine,* "Where Have All the Ulcers Gone?"[3] Mr. Baker pointed out that people seemed to get fewer ulcers these days. His article set me to speculating that since everyone, doctors and layman alike, had come to realize that ulcers really meant tension, they no longer served the purpose of hiding tension, so fewer people developed ulcers. Could this be the reason why neck, shoulder and back pains have become so common in recent years? Is it possible that these are now much better hiding places for tension than the stomach?

There is another bit of evidence that psychological and not structural factors are responsible for back pain. One of the common manifestations of TMS that people find perplexing is the occurrence of pain at night. Some are awakened out of a sound sleep by pain, usually attributing it to having turned over, but most patients are mystified, having been told that rest in bed was the appropriate treatment for back pain. Presumably the rationale for bed rest is to relieve the spine of its weight-bearing job, thereby eliminating the pain. Why then do many patients have their most painful hours during the night?

Tension resides in the unconscious mind, and unconscious mental activity never ceases. For some people with TMS, apparently the tension level rises while they sleep, and the result is an increase in pain. There appears to be a direct relationship between the level of tension and the degree of pain, which I have observed firsthand both in myself and in patients.

Having myself a compulsive, perfectionistic personality, I have experienced many physical manifestations of tension through the years, including TMS in the shoulders and in the low back. For two summers in succession I developed acute sciatica due to TMS and never realized until the end of the second summer that it was related to tennis. I had just taken up the game for the first time and was so intent on becoming an instant champion that I generated quantities of tension. Most of the pain occurred at night, which is my pattern.

I have had an opportunity to observe TMS closely in patients in the hospital, and clearly the degree of pain they suffer measures their levels of tension. For example, a patient will receive an upsetting telephone call from a family member, and two hours later the pain becomes excruciating.

To reiterate, the level of tension determines when and how severely one will have pain. What remains a mystery is why the level of tension rises at night for some people and not for others. TMS varies in severity from very mild to totally disabling; the majority are somewhere between, with varying degrees of disability.

A number of years ago, when the details of TMS were just beginning to emerge from my studies, I searched the medical literature for some confirmation of my observations. It seemed inconceivable to me that this condition had never been described before. I was gratified when I found an article in a 1946 issue of the *New England Journal of Medicine*.[4] The article was written by a doctor from Boston, Maj. Morgan Sargent, who at the time was assigned to an Army Air Force convalescent hospital in St. Petersburg, Florida. Dr. Sargent described a large population of returning Air Force personnel with complaints of backache. Of the many young men he evaluated he found that less than 4 percent had back pain that could be attributed to a structural problem alone. The rest had pain that was exclusively or predominantly the result of psychological factors. As I read the paper with growing excitement I realized that what he was describing was TMS. He talked about muscular tension as the physical manifestation of increased nervous tension. His case histories illustrated a number of typical TMS patterns of back pain, showing how patients commonly attribute the onset of symptoms to an injury, often remote in time. He described how the trouble often began in association with some anxiety-producing situation. The great variability of symptoms was described as well as the important observation by one patient that when his back pain disappeared he experienced extreme anxiety.

The discovery of this paper came at an important moment for me. I needed the reassurance that someone else had observed these phenomena in much the same way I had.

Subsequently I found another paper, written by Drs. Holmes and Wolff, both well-known pioneers in the study of pain, that related life situations, emotions and backache.[5] From this paper came the idea that reduced blood circulation might be the physical basis for the pain.

THE PHYSICAL BASIS FOR THE PAIN OF TMS

The brain is the most complex organ in the body and the one we know least about. It is what most identifies us as human, for it is the repository of thought, language and emotion. The functions we share with lower animals, such as walking, digesting and excreting, are much simpler to understand; the ones that make us uniquely human are the most difficult and, indeed, remain obscure to this day. For this reason we are unable to describe the exact process that produces TMS. However, because we may not know the details of a process does not mean that we cannot observe the process itself. This is the case with TMS; it begins in the brain, and that is where we must look first.

Deep in the brain lie groups of nerve cells that comprise the "limbic system." This system has a great deal to do with the emotions. Figure 5 shows the approximate location of these "emotion centers."

Nearby are other groups of cells that control all the involuntary functions of the body, such as tearing, salivation, breathing, the heartbeat, digestive activity, urinary and sexual function and of greatest interest to us here, the blood supply to all parts

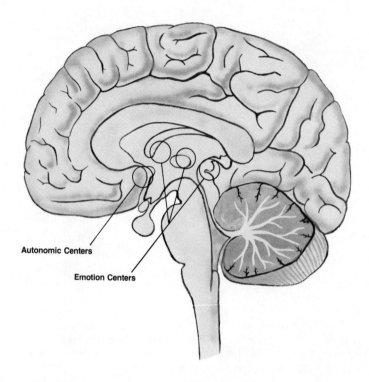

Autonomic Centers

Emotion Centers

Figure 5. **This drawing of the brain identifies the location of so-called emotion centers and autonomic centers**

of the body. This is known as the *autonomic nervous system,* and its centers of origin are also identified in Figure 5.

Figure 6 illustrates how messages that originate in the brain's autonomic centers travel down through the spinal cord and exit from the cord over a network of nerves to various organs of the body. It is the purpose of this system to keep all the organs and systems of the body operating optimally under a variety of circumstances ranging from everyday functions to extreme emergencies. The autonomic centers of the brain respond to a great

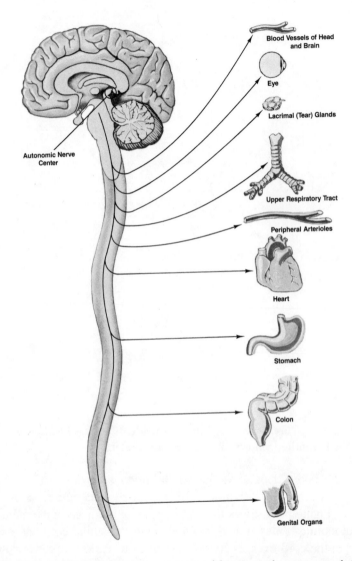

Figure 6. Autonomic nervous system with connections to a variety of organs, including arterioles. The arterioles are the targets for tension which results in the circulatory changes that cause the pain of TMS

variety of stimuli to keep the body functioning properly. For example, under conditions of extreme cold the autonomic centers will signal the partial shutting down of blood vessels in the skin, which results in heat preservation. Conversely, in hot weather these same blood vessels will be opened up, allowing a greater amount of blood to flow through the skin, thereby dissipating heat.

Although many of the stimuli that cause the autonomic centers to react are physical, such as heat, cold, hunger and fatigue, emotions are important stimulators as well. When we are sad, saline fluid is made to flow from the tear glands; anger causes the eyes to open wide, a faster heartbeat, tense muscles, etc.; fear prepares the whole body to run or fight, via the autonomic system. All animals experience this, but because human beings are more complicated, they have a broader repertoire of emotions; tension is one of these. Under artificial situations some animals can be made tense and anxious, but for human beings tension is part of everyday life, and excesses of it can produce physical disorders, of which TMS is probably now the most common.

With this introduction we can now look at the specific physiology of the tension myositis syndrome. The autonomic nervous system controls the circulation of blood all over the body. Blood is pumped from the heart into a system of large blood vessels, the arteries, which then divide and subdivide into progressively smaller units until, at the tissue level, the blood is carried through small blood vessels called arterioles to all parts of the body. The autonomic nervous system determines whether a given part of the body—the muscles of the buttocks, for example—will have a normal, increased or decreased amount of blood at any given moment. Changes in local circulation will occur as a result of such things as heat and cold, physical activity or fear and anxiety. These changes are all brought about through the action of the autonomic system.

TMS is the result of tension-induced alterations in local circulation resulting in blood deprivation, called *ischemia*. Tension causes the arterioles to close partly (vasoconstriction), and this slows the circulation of blood in a given area, thereby depriving the tissues of their normal blood supply. Though any of the muscles of the neck, shoulders and back may be involved, there appears to be a hierarchy of favored pain sites. The upper-outer buttocks are the most commonly involved, while the top of the shoulders and sides of the neck are next in order of frequency.

This blood deprivation is *not* sufficient to damage the muscles and nerves except infrequently; still, back pain is almost always associated with damage or injury to structures in the back. A similar benign condition occurs when the body is exposed to cold temperatures. There is vasoconstriction and a diminished blood supply, but it is part of the body's normal regulating mechanisms. When the temperature increases, the blood supply will be increased; when tension is alleviated, the arterioles will open.

Figure 7 shows that the inner half of the buttock receives its normal complement of blood while the outer half is deprived of a normal amount because of constriction of the blood vessels serving the area. The resultant pain is due, first, to an accumulation of chemical waste products in the muscle. These chemicals ordinarily are carried away by the blood and eliminated or detoxified in other parts of the body. The sluggish circulation allows them to build up; they are depicted as black dots in the drawing.

Second, reduced circulation means that insufficient oxygen reaches the muscle, causing it to spasm. Back muscle spasm is similar to calf muscle cramps (charley horse), which are familiar to everyone. Unlike calf cramps, which quickly stop, back or neck muscle spasms persist. It is common for episodes of TMS to begin with such spasms, which may totally immobilize the individual.

Third, reduced circulation results in reduced oxygen to nerves such as the sciatic in the buttock, spinal nerves in the low back and neck, and the brachial plexus. These are known as peripheral nerves. Their response to lowered levels of oxygen is pain;

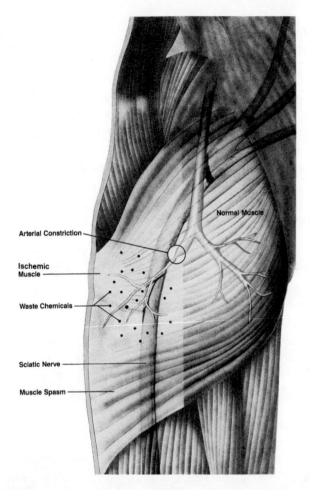

Figure 7. **This drawing illustrates the three reasons for pain resulting from ischemia: (1) Muscle spasm, (2) accumulated chemical wastes, and (3) nerve pain**

if the oxygen level is lower still, there may be feelings of numbness, ''pins and needles'' and even reduced strength in muscles. The latter is rare in TMS; when it occurs it means that some of the motor nerve fibers bringing messages from the brain have been damaged.

Because of their location in the buttocks, the peripheral nerves most often subjected to oxygen deprivation in TMS are the sciatic nerves (one on each side). They serve most of the legs. When the spinal nerves of the neck and the brachial plexus are implicated, pain in the arms and hands results.

Nerves bring messages to and from the brain, serving all parts of the body. When any nerve is irritated or damaged, as by oxygen deprivation, pain will be felt wherever that nerve is going or, to put it another way, in the part of the body being served by the nerve. In short, oxygen deprivation of nerves produces the leg and arm pain of TMS.

It is important to reiterate that tension can produce a variety of physical reactions through the autonomic nervous system, of which TMS is the most common. These reactions appear to be interchangeable so that one may have heartburn, for example, or symptoms of tension headache instead of TMS. This has important implications for treatment, as we shall see later on.

To summarize, most neck, shoulder and back pain is due to TMS, a harmless physical disorder of the muscles and nerves that is most immediately due to reduced blood circulation to these tissues. This circulatory abnormality results from constriction of the small blood vessels that feed the involved tissues; the constriction is brought about by tension. Tension, in turn, is primarily the result of certain personality characteristics and is often increased by real-life situations.

Although human beings have always generated tension in the struggle to survive and progress, contemporary life is particularly tension-producing. We can do very little about the social patterns responsible for this, but by intelligent reflection we can see to it that tension does not cause the physical reactions described above. Following a more complete description of TMS in the next chapter I shall describe how we go about eliminating the symptoms of neck, shoulder or back pain.

Chapter 4
The Manifestations of TMS

Most patients I have seen believed that their pain was due to an injury brought on by a physical incident. These varied from lifting a heavy object to a minor automobile accident, most commonly the hit-from-behind type. At some point after the accident—minutes, hours or days—the neck or back pain started, and so the patient made the "obvious" connection.

Some of the reported physical incidents were trivial, raising an important question: How can severe back pain be started by incidents so variable in severity? I recall a man of twenty-eight who was sitting at his desk writing. He relaxed in his chair for a moment and when he leaned forward to resume writing experienced an excruciating spasm in the low back, so severe and persistent that he had to be taken home by ambulance. Once home he spent an agonizing forty-eight hours during which he could not move without settting off a new wave of spasm, despite a variety of medications. What does that insignificant movement at his desk have in common with a rear-end auto accident, a swing at a golf ball, a slip on the ice or lifting a garbage can? In my view they are all *triggers* and have nothing to do with the basic cause of pain.

In 1978 I surveyed a group of a hundred TMS patients with regard to how their pain started. The results are in Table 1. Sixty percent reported that when the pain began it was *not* associated with a physical incident! They awakened one morning and it was

Table 1   *How Pain Began in 100 Patients with TMS*

1. Gradual (no physical incident)	60%
2. Sudden onset (a physical incident)	40%
a. Accident or injury	18%
b. Strain, lift, push, pull	8%
c. Twist or bend	10%
d. Other	4%

there or it gradually came on during the day. However, all of those patients tried to recall something physical that had happened, sometimes going back twenty or thirty years, because they thought there *had to be* such an incident, since everything they had heard about back pain related it to an injury and a *structural* problem.

It was clear from their histories that there could be no possible relationship between those remote physical incidents and the onset of pain.

As can be seen in Table 1, 40 percent of the patients did report something physical at onset, but when I reviewed subsequent events in the histories of all hundred patients there was no correlation between how the pain began and its severity or longevity. That is, some patients whose pain started gradually later developed severe pain, and some whose pain started with physical incidents had mild symptoms subsequently.

There seemed to be only one logical conclusion: Physical incidents did not cause the pain but acted as a *trigger*. The process of TMS probably exists in back muscles for months or years before the pain begins, but in a milder state. Then at some critical point with a small increase in severity (the straw and the camel's back), the pain begins. In 40 percent of cases the onset of pain is associated with a physical occurrence, and in 60 percent it appears to come out of nowhere. Lending further credence to the idea of a trigger mechanism, patients commonly reported that subsequent attacks of pain sometimes began with a physical incident and sometimes not.

Another argument against attributing persistent pain to a physical incident is that breaks, tears, sprains or strains heal in a matter of days or weeks. It is illogical to blame such injuries for continuing pain.

Establishing the significance of initial physical incidents is important because it bears so heavily on the cause of the back pain and, therefore, the "cure." In my experience, patients who are convinced that they have "injured" their back will continue to have pain. If they can be made aware that tension is responsible and that they need not fear physical activity, the problem can be resolved.

Once they realize that an injury or spinal abnormality is not the cause of the pain, patients often relate the onset of pain to a psychological factor—for example, a new job, a "pressure cooker" atmosphere at work, illness in the family, marital or parent-child problems, financial difficulties, etc. At that point they will usually acknowledge that they tend to be tense or excessively conscientious, overly responsible or "a worrier." Some recognize that they are compulsive or perfectionistic. Some, of course, strongly maintain that tension could not possibly cause the pain. Some remain recalcitrant and fail to improve; others eventually accept the diagnosis as they learn more about it, and then are able to improve.

TMS AND MUSCLES

Where do patients feel pain? As described in the preceding chapter, TMS results from mild blood deprivation in muscles and nerves of the neck, shoulders, back and buttocks. The muscles are shown in Figure 8. The drawing also shows the two areas most frequently involved—the low back-buttock region, and the neck-shoulder and upper back.

Table 2 shows the specific areas designated as the primary pain site in a hundred TMS patients; Table 3 indicates the painful places reported by the same group of patients.

These figures will not be surprising to back pain sufferers. Almost two thirds identified the buttocks as the primary site—

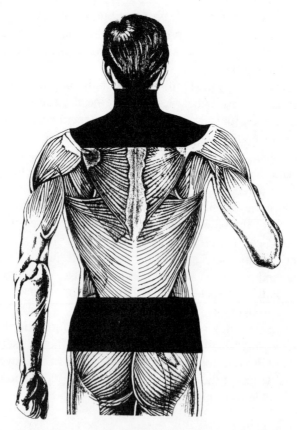

Figure 8. **A drawing of the postural muscles of the neck, shoulders and back. It also indicates which muscles are most susceptible to TMS**

that is, anywhere in the buttock including the side, which patients often referred to as the hip. Some people were under the impression that something was wrong with the hip joint and often were not reassured that it was normal without an X ray. In 28 percent the primary problem was somewhere in the neck, top of the shoulders or upper back (usually around the shoulder blades), and often when there was pain in one of these areas there was a good deal in the others too. As you can see, the "small of the

Table 2   *Major Pain Locations for 100 Patients with TMS*

Buttock	60%
Shoulder	12%
Neck	9%
Lumbar	8%
Thoracic	7%
Other	4%

Table 3   *Pain Locations for 100 Patients with TMS*

Left buttock	67%	Left neck	30%
Right buttock	68%	Right neck	33%
Left lumbar	34%	Left shoulder	33%
Right lumbar	36%	Right shoulder	36%
Midlumbar	9%	Left thoracic	15%
Midthoracic	. 2%	Right thoracic	15%

Both upper and lower back	44%
Both sides lower back	61%

back'' (lumbar) was not often the primary location, though as noted in Table 3, over a third of the patients reported some pain in the lumbar area.

Substantial numbers reported pain on both sides in the low back-buttock area (61 percent) and pain in both the upper and lower back (44 percent). These figures are important, for they make it difficult to attribute the pain to a herniated lumbar disc or "pinched nerve" in the neck, the two most common structural diagnoses. Most structural problems cause pain in a single location and are limited to one side of the body.

The very common "stiff neck" is caused by TMS in neck muscles but does not worry people as low back pain does. Most automatically relate it to tension.

Beyond identifying the various sites of TMS pain, the statistics in Tables 2 and 3 help to establish the concept that TMS is a *syndrome*—that is, a combination of symptoms that occur together. For example, if many postural muscles are involved, this indicates that the patient suffers from the tension myositis syndrome. By contrast, structural abnormalities produce isolated symptoms. Pain in multiple sites simultaneously attributed to a single structural abnormality makes little sense.

TMS AND NERVES

The most common result of nerve involvement with TMS is pain, and the most common locations for that pain are the legs and arms, in that order. This is logical, since the postural muscles in the buttock and neck-shoulder regions are most susceptible to TMS, and their nerves appear to be implicated by virtue of their locations in or near these muscles. The relevant anatomy of these regions was described in Chapter 3, demonstrating how the sciatic nerves in the buttocks and the spinal nerves and brachial plexus in the neck-shoulder area come to be involved.

The occurrence of nerve pain in the legs or arms is an invariably frightening component of TMS. Patients associate it with nerve damage by a structural injury, and it conjures up images of deterioration and more serious consequences to come. They have learned, too, that surgery is frequently recommended for people with nerve pain. This increases anxiety and, therefore, intensifies and perpetuates the pain.

Though less frequent, leg pain can be caused by lumbar spinal as well as sciatic nerve involvement.

Nerve pain can involve any part of the legs or arms, the pattern varying considerably. For example, one patient may have only thigh or foot pain; another, pain in the calf of the leg. In some the pain radiates down the entire leg. The same holds true for the arms. The quality of the pain varies, too: It may be burning, aching or shooting. Although it tends to involve one limb at a time, some patients have it in both arms or legs; at other times it alternates.

Variability of symptoms is characteristic of TMS and helps

to establish the diagnosis. Since the pain is due to tension, and since people's level of tension varies from day to day, sometimes from hour to hour, it is logical that the pain will also vary. On the other hand, if the pain were due to a structural abnormality, such as an arthritic spur, one would expect it to be the same all the time.

In addition to pain, oxygen deprivation may cause other nerve symptoms, most commonly feelings of numbness and/or tingling in the legs or arms. These, too, frighten patients and aggravate the problem. Less frequently, there is a reduction in amplitude or absence of a reflex reaction when the tendons of the knees or ankles are tapped with a rubber hammer. This indicates that the process is more severe but is still not cause for alarm. Even greater severity is signaled by the loss of strength in some part of a leg or arm, but this is rare.

Part of the physical examination is to determine whether there is any evidence of nerve damage. In addition to testing the reflexes and muscle strength of the arms and legs, nerve transmission of sensory messages to the brain is recorded by testing skin sensitivity to pin prick. Minor reductions in sensitivity are quite common with TMS.

A common symptom of nerve involvement in the neck-shoulder region is pain in the upper part of the arm near the shoulder joint, sometimes leading to partial "freezing" of the joint. This is usually diagnosed as bursitis. Similarly, chest pain or abdominal pain may result from TMS-induced nerve irritation of spinal nerves in the upper and middle back. In each case it is important that the patient be made aware of the correct diagnosis, since all these symptoms are routinely eliminated with proper TMS treatment.

MUSCLE PAIN ON PRESSURE

The patterns of spontaneous pain in the postural areas and limbs just described are convincing evidence that TMS is the cause of most neck, shoulder and back pain. More convincing, however, was the discovery that TMS involves many more muscles than those that hurt spontaneously. During the 1978 statistical survey to document the characteristics of TMS, it was decided that the physical examination would include testing all the postural muscles for tenderness on pressure. Previously this had been done only where the patient complained of pain. Two things emerged: First, many postural muscles were painful on pressure, though the patient was aware of no pain otherwise; second, there was a definite *pattern* of muscle involvement, regardless of where the primary site of pain was.

These points will be clear by looking at the figures in Table 4.

Table 4   *Tenderness on Palpation for 100 Patients with TMS*

Left neck	67%	Left thoracic	12%
Right neck	83%	Right thoracic	13%
Left shoulder	72%	Left lumbar	45%
Right shoulder	83%	Right lumbar	46%
Left buttock	77%		
Right buttock	78%	Both buttocks	76%

Simultaneous right neck, right shoulder and right gluteal	71%

The table shows that 71 percent of the group were simultaneously tender to pressure over the right side of the neck, right top of the shoulder and right buttock, *regardless* of where the major pain was. I concluded that all of the postural muscles are targets for tension but that some are more susceptible than others (see Figure 8). Perhaps the explanation for this is that the most important postural muscles are the ones most frequently involved. Note the high proportion of patients with buttock tenderness: 77 percent on the left and 78 percent on the right. The buttock muscles keep the trunk upright on the legs, a very important job. The neck muscles keep the head erect on the trunk, and the muscles at the top of the shoulders stabilize the arms so that they can be used properly; if the shoulder muscles are not functioning properly, arm function will be severely curtailed. The higher numbers involving the right neck and shoulder may have something to do with the fact that most of us are right-handed.

The importance of this pain on pressure cannot be overemphasized. Muscle tenderness on pressure is the hallmark of TMS; it is the only objective evidence of the alteration in muscle physiology brought about by TMS. It explains the "trigger points" that doctors have been talking about for years, which can now be recognized as the central zone of a wider area of muscle pain induced by blood deprivation.

Only the postural muscles and their associated nerves are targets for TMS; the muscles of the arms and legs are not similarly involved. This is a clinical fact, similar to the fact that the stomach or colon may be a target organ for tension, so it is not necessary to know why. One wonders, however, if the nature of their work is what makes postural muscles selectively susceptible to TMS. Because they are responsible for maintaining head and trunk posture and supporting the arms at the shoulders, they are constantly active during one's waking hours and, therefore, perhaps more subject to fatigue than the muscles of the arms and legs.

The Symptoms of TMS

The pain of TMS varies widely in quality, since there are three reasons for it: muscle spasm, accumulated chemical wastes and nerve irritation. An acute attack is characterized by sharp, excruciating pain due to the sudden onset of muscle spasm. The pain is so severe that patients invariably conclude that something structural and catastrophic has occurred and make statements such as "My back went out" or "Something snapped." In fact, it is highly unlikely that a structural derangement could produce pain equal in severity to acute muscle spasm. Their pain may continue for days, weeks or months, depending on the patient's subsequent course.

The accumulation of chemical wastes causes pain of a duller, aching quality that will also persist as long as the circulatory insufficiency remains, though varying in intensity. Nerve pain may be burning, aching or shooting.

TMS muscles are sore from blood deprivation; they are not infected or inflamed. They feel as though they are because of the soreness. This is responsible for many of the symptoms of TMS. For example, TMS in the buttocks makes sitting very painful. Active contraction, which is how muscles work, also causes pain in a sore muscle, as does stretching the muscle. Many patients, therefore, complain of increased pain with standing in one place (active contraction without movement). Bending over at the waist or elevating an extended leg while lying down also stretches involved muscles and causes pain. These maneuvers also illustrate the principle that stretching a TMS-involved nerve also causes pain, in this case of the sciatic nerve.

Patients with TMS consistently report that moist heat (moist packs, hot shower, hot tub) relieves pain and sometimes dispels it completely for short periods of time. This supports the concept that TMS is due to reduced blood circulation, since heat probably works by improving the local circulation. The pain, however, invariably returns because the process is governed by the *brain* and not by what is done locally. Conversely, cold generally increases pain in TMS muscles by further slowing the circulation.

Exercise also improves circulation in muscles but whether it is effective in easing pain depends on what patients believe. Patients who have learned to fear exercise will not benefit from it. The final determinant of whether there will be pain is the degree of tension; fear increases tension, and patients with TMS invariably learn to fear many things, as described earlier. Pain automatically starts or becomes worse in response to many physical activities or maneuvers. Sometimes just *thinking* about an activity is enough to start the pain.

THE NATURAL HISTORY OF TMS

There is no such thing as a typical back pain history, but certain patterns are very common. Perhaps the most consistent is the tendency for the pain to recur. Once an individual has experienced neck, shoulder or back pain, it will come back, though not always in the same place or in the same way, regardless of type or length of treatment. This is true for patients who have had surgery as well, though some have a reprieve of a year or two. Very rarely does one hear of someone who never has pain again after surgery. The majority continue to have a problem, and some get worse.

At the beginning the attacks may be infrequent, the second attack sometimes occurring as long as five or ten years later. Gradually painful episodes recur more frequently, especially if there is an impressive physical incident along the way, suggesting to the patient that something is now seriously wrong with the back. As the attacks become more frequent they last longer and do not respond to the usual measures (a day in bed, aspirin, hot showers, etc.). Eventually many patients reach the point where they always have pain somewhere in the neck, shoulders, low back or upper buttock; often they complain of pain at the tip of the spine.

This chronic pain takes several patterns; many patients report having a lot of trouble for the first few hours of the day, then gradually "loosening up." Others are fairly comfortable in the morning but get worse as the day wears on. Regardless of the pattern, all have a list of things they can and cannot do. Even after developing a chronic pattern, most patients continue to have acute attacks, of which they live in dread, for they are usually characterized by excruciating pain (severe muscle spasm), trunk deformities (can't straighten up or trunk tilted to one side) and severe disability.

The tendency to recurrence and chronicity can be only partially attributed to the underlying causes of the pain: personality and tension. Having been told that there is something structurally wrong with the back, patients live in constant fear of an acute attack, avoiding activities that might possibly "reinjure" the back. The result is increased tension, which feeds into the reservoir and helps to perpetuate the process. The structural diagnosis and everything that flows from that misdiagnosis is a major reason for the gradual worsening of the condition. Thus the need for reeducation of both patient and physician.

There is pain at other sites in the arms or legs; such pains frequently occur simultaneously with TMS and are not due to nerve involvement. It is important to mention them because many of them are thought to be due to inflammatory processes and are not generally related to buttock, back, neck or shoulder pain. The most common of these are various forms of tendinitis, the best known of which is the so-called "tennis elbow" (lateral epicondylitis). Pain occurs at the point of attachment of an important tendon to a bony protuberance at the elbow. Also fairly common is tendinitis at the knee and ankle, particularly the Achilles tendon.

I have observed that the pain from these conditions often disappears when patients are treated successfully for TMS. Though the mechanism is not clear, it has happened so frequently that I believe there is a relationship between these disorders and TMS.

In considering the natural history of TMS, it is instructive to consider the age distribution of the disorder. At what ages is TMS most prevalent?

In the summer of 1982, in preparation for this book, a follow-up study was conducted to document the results of my treatment program. One hundred seventy-seven patients were interviewed, on whom outcome data are presented in Chapter 5. Of interest to us here is the age distribution of the patient sample, which is representative of patients I have treated through the years.

The bar graph in Figure 9 gives the age breakdown by decade. Seventy-seven percent of the group fell between the ages of thirty and fifty-nine. Note that there are fewer patients in their

Figure 9

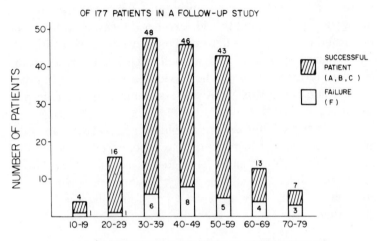

AGE DISTRIBUTION

OF 177 PATIENTS IN A FOLLOW-UP STUDY

sixties than in their twenties! Since the majority of back pain syndromes are attributed to degenerative processes—for example, degenerative osteoarthritis and degenerative disc disease—it is strange, indeed, that there were only thirteen patients aged sixty to sixty-nine and seven in their seventies.

A study published in a Canadian medical journal confirms this age distribution for back pain. The authors reported that 60 percent of twenty-two hundred back pain patients were between thirty and fifty years of age; 25 percent were over fifty and 15 percent under thirty.[1]

What these data confirm is that degenerative processes have nothing to do with most back pain. Degeneration is progressive and relentless; serial X rays as one ages document this fact. Yet back pain is far less common in the older age groups. According to the conventional diagnostic concepts, everyone over the age of sixty should have back pain.

The age statistics are helpful not only as evidence against

the structural diagnoses but also because they give a straightforward indication of what the correct diagnosis might be. The years from thirty to sixty are certainly the most eventful in most people's lives. We may be very busy between the ages of ten and thirty, but life is less serious during that time. The transition to the world of responsibility adds another dimension to life—one that invariably generates tension. People whose personalities do not demand responsible behavior will not generate much tension and will not experience psychophysiological reactions, but they are not numerous. Most of us possess elements of the TMS personality.

Though predominant in the middle years, TMS can occur at any age. I have had patients who experienced it for the first time in their eighties, and I have good reason to believe that it occurs in children, though as with many disorders common to all ages, looking very different. The following may be enlightening.

TMS IN CHILDREN

I practiced as a family physician for nine years after graduating from medical school. Like all family doctors, I often saw children who were brought in by their mothers because of mysterious pains, usually in the legs, that sometimes were severe and frightening. These children were invariably found to be healthy, and I was forced to fall back on the tried and true diagnosis of "growing pains." No one seems to have identified the nature of these mysterious pains.

One night my own young daughter awakened crying with pain in the calf of one of her legs. I reassured her and my wife that this was probably "growing pains." As I sat on her bed waiting for the pain to subside it occurred to me that calf pain could very well be sciatic pain. Examination did, indeed, reveal that there was tenderness in the buttock, from which I concluded that the pain probably was sciatic in origin and that she was having a manifestation of acute TMS.

We forget that children build up tensions just as adults do, and children's tensions often are manifest at night while they sleep. Young and old alike have nightmares, which are the subconscious expression of fears and concerns generated during the day or carried over from an earlier experience. It would not be inappropriate to characterize a child's nocturnal attack of TMS as a nightmare equivalent.

Armed with this information, the basic treatment for my daughter was much the same as that which Grandmother would have employed: reassurance, comfort. The modern treatment I added was some gentle massage of the tender area in the buttock.

We are psychological beings from the day we are born until the day we die. We react emotionally throughout this span and are capable of experiencing physical reactions based on emotion during our entire lives. The age statistics reinforce the concept that neck, shoulder and back pain are tension-induced.

There is another interesting phenomenon that demonstrates the relationship between tension and TMS. In patients with very severe TMS, those we generally treat in the hospital, it has been observed that there is often a reciprocal relationship between the awareness of tension and the pain. That is to say, if the patient was aware of *feeling* very tense on a particular day, he or she had less pain. On the other hand, if he or she was feeling calm, the pain was usually more severe. It demonstrated very clearly that the tension felt (experienced as an emotion) was not diverted into the muscles; conversely, if the patient didn't feel it emotionally, it was felt in the back. I have made this observation repeatedly. Ms. C. reports, "I worked on some very painful things with my psychologist yesterday, things that I hated to think and talk about and I realized at the end of the session that I had no pain."

For this reason I teach my patients to think of their pain in *psychological terms,* for if they can do that, the tension will cease to produce a *physical reaction;* it will be manifest in the emotions, where it belongs, and not in the back, where it is inappropriate—where it is hiding, so to speak.

THE WISDOM OF NATURE

The wisdom of nature is expressed in many ways, among the most impressive of which are the elaborate mechanisms for healing built into all living things. The advances of modern medical science have obscured this fundamental fact, for physicians have been so preoccupied with their own investigative and therapeutic efforts that they have failed to recognize the power of some of nature's processes. Consequently they have not made them part of their therapeutic approach.

TMS and all other psychophysiological disorders are good examples of this. I have learned in working with TMS that human beings have great capacities for self-healing; but those powers must be recognized and unleashed. A physician should facilitate patient awareness and utilization of nature's self-restorative processes. I believe that my TMS patients cure themselves once I have provided them with the proper information. In my view this is the best medicine: releasing the potential within individuals to heal themselves.

Chapter 5
The Treatment of TMS

The treatment of TMS evolved from my observations of patients reacting to traditional treatment, and from my gradual realization of why some patients got better and others didn't.

I have always explained to patients in considerable detail the nature of their illnesses or problems. When I began to make the diagnosis of TMS there was an even stronger compulsion to do this because of the unusual nature of the disorder and my desire to reassure patients that they did not have serious structural abnormalities. Out of this practice came the awareness that the patients who got better *accepted* the diagnosis; patients who rejected the idea of tension as the basis for their pain improved little or not at all.

Surely this is a remarkable phenomenon. How can knowing about and accepting the diagnosis of TMS bring about a "cure"?

In Chapter 3 I suggested that psychophysiologic reactions such as ulcer, migraine and TMS seem to be an attempt by the mind to discharge excess tension in a way that masks or hides the tension. I said that this subterfuge is necessary because obvious manifestations of tension are acceptable neither to the individual nor to society. Quite unconsciously, we prefer not to be considered nervous or jittery. I suggested that stomach ulcers occur less often now because it became common knowledge that

ulcers were due to tension; the subterfuge was revealed, and ulcers became a less acceptable outlet for tension.

When I observed that patient awareness of the details of TMS
could banish the pain, I concluded that this was similar to what
seems to have occurred with stomach ulcers—that is, once people realized that their back pain was due to tension and not a
structural abnormality, it stopped.

What is responsible for this remarkable phenomenon? Is it
that we have raised the problem from the unconscious to the
conscious level of thought, exposing the true nature of the process? Whatever the brain mechanism, it is quite clear that the
knowledge of what is going on prevents the autonomic nervous
system from transmitting nerve messages that constrict the blood
vessels and cause muscle and nerve pain.

I believe that patient knowledge of the nature and cause of
their symptoms has the power to abort any psychophysiologic
reaction. An experience I had many years ago is pertinent. I used
to have migraine headaches regularly when I first started to
practice medicine. They were the classic type: The sick headache was preceded by blurred vision about fifteen minutes earlier. One day a psychiatrist friend told me that there was a theory
that migraines were due to repressed anger and that I should think
about this the next time I got my visual warning. I did so and
to my astonishment did not develop a headache. I have never
had another migraine headache, though I continued to experience occasional blurred vision through the years. This is a very
clear example of how mental activity can stop a psychophysiologic reaction.

When patients are presented with the diagnosis of TMS they
usually conclude that it will be necessary to reduce or eliminate
tension to get rid of the pain. This seems logical, and without
doubt a significant reduction in tension would abolish the pain.
But reducing the tension in one's life is very difficult if not impossible, because tension is so much the result of personality traits
and temperament. Tension is also due to stressful life circumstances, and changing these may not be possible. One can't sim-

ply leave a pressure-filled job. And what do you do if you have a sick child, or one with other problems? There is always tension.

Patients then suggest that their tension may be relieved in other ways, such as through meditation, Yoga, relaxation exercise or aerobic exercise. Don't these reduce tension? They do, but in my experience not nearly enough to eliminate TMS. Many patients had tried these methods before I treated them, with no significant reduction in back pain.

Logic suggests to patients yet another possibility. Perhaps as their back pain departs, the tension will find a different target and cause some other physical disorder, such as an ulcer. Fortunately, we found that this did not happen either, though it is quite common when symptoms are removed by other forms of treatment; this is known as symptom substitution.

Here then is a strange situation: The tension is not relieved by changes in personality or circumstance, relaxation or transference to another part of the body. And yet the pain departs. Why?

Perhaps the question can be answered by looking at an analogous situation. People with an irrational fear (phobia) that results from extreme tension (anxiety) lose the phobia when they discover the true source of the fear. For example, a woman suddenly developed a morbid fear of riding on the subway, though she had done it all her life. In exploring the problem with a psychotherapist she recalled eventually that the last time she had ridden on the subway she had seen a newspaper headline about a mother who injured her infant child. Apparently this stimulated a long-held guilt about one of her children, arousing a great deal of anxiety and resulting in the subway phobia. By talking it through with her psychotherapist the guilty feelings about her child were put into proper perspective; the anxiety diminished and the phobia disappeared.

With the TMS patient it is likely that simply confronting the fact that tension can produce back pain somehow reduces the tension and therefore the pain. It is further reduced when the patient is reassured that the pain is not due to a structural abnormality.

It is also possible that since the tension is masquerading as a physical symptom, it will cease to do so when the deception has been exposed. That is to say, once the patient becomes aware that tension is the source of the pain, the process will have lost its reason for being.

These are speculations, an attempt to explain something that has been repeatedly observed. We shall not know what happens to the tension until we know a great deal more about how the brain works. What is clear is that though the mind can cause undesirable reactions such as TMS, it also has the power to eliminate those reactions through thought and reflection. Indeed, if this were not true I would have had no success in the treatment of TMS. What we observed instead was that understanding and accepting the diagnosis of TMS was equivalent to "cure" in the majority of cases.

Before going on to a description of the actual programs of treatment for TMS it might be helpful to consider other examples of how the mind can affect the body.

One of the most celebrated medical experiences of recent years was described in a book entitled *Anatomy of an Illness* by well-known literary figure Norman Cousins.[1] Deep in the throes of a serious disease that was eroding most of the joints in his body, he concluded at the eleventh hour that he personally must assume an active role in his treatment. He decided that negative emotions had played a key part in producing his illness and, if that was the case, there must be a place for positive emotions in his treatment. With the help of his family physician he proceeded to act on those assumptions and set up a program to implement his conclusions. The result is that he experienced a remarkable turnabout in the course of his illness and slowly and progressively got better. Mr. Cousins concedes that the explanation for his recovery cannot be conclusively explained on the basis of present medical knowledge. Yet the recovery was surely effected by the power of his own mind. That conclusion is generally accepted by the medical community. In my view, it was Mr. Cousins' realization of the role of emotional factors in producing his illness which permitted his body to throw it off. I believe it was his *awareness* of this fact plus the conviction that he could do something about the problem that were the crucial factors in his recovery. This goes beyond the placebo effect, since placebos depend on blind faith. Mr. Cousins' faith was not blind; he believed in the ability of the mind to heal and knew that he must play an active role in mobilizing that potential.

A patient with low back pain who believes that there is some *structural* abnormality of the spine causing the pain and who gets better as a result of some form of treatment is experiencing a placebo effect. Therefore, it can be expected that the symptoms will return, and they usually do. If, on the other hand, the patient concludes that the process in the back muscles is due to tension, that there is nothing to fear and that the patient can contribute to his or her own recovery, then the result is a permanent cure.

THE WITCH DOCTOR

I found another excellent example of mind-body interaction in an article by an engineer and explorer, Louis C. Whiton, in the magazine *Natural History*.[2] Dr. Whiton had been conducting anthropological studies in Surinam, South America, for many years and was particularly interested in the ceremonies, rituals and cures of tribal witch doctors from a group of jungle people known as Bush Negroes. He had been suffering for two years from a painful condition of the right leg and hip attributed to trochanteric bursitis, which had been resistant to all treatment. Consequently he decided to try his luck with one of the witch doctors and sought out a man named Raineh. Dr. Whiton was accompanied by his personal physician, five friends and the editor of a Surinamese newspaper; they traveled into the forest about forty miles from Paramaribo for the treatment.

The ceremony began at midnight and continued until four-thirty in the morning and is described in great detail by Dr. Whiton. The process included many steps, whose purposes were to protect the patient from evil spirits, interrogate his soul about his past life, attract beneficent local gods and "pull the witch" out of his body and transfer it to that of the witch doctor. At this point in the ceremony Dr. Whiton arose from the ground and found that his pain had disappeared.

There were further rituals in which the "witch" had to be exorcised from the body of the doctor and transferred to the body of a chicken, which then died. The ceremony concluded with incantations and other procedures to prevent the "evil" from reentering his body.

One is forced to certain conclusions: In all likelihood Dr. Whiton did not have trochanteric bursitis; he was probably suffering from the tension myositis syndrome. In that case any treatment that made a strong enough impact on his mind could be successful. The witch doctor was an imposing, self-confident, intensely serious man, and he obviously impressed Dr. Whiton. What is probably more important, the author believed in the power of the mind to heal the body; apparently the witch doctor's ceremony provided the mechanism to actualize that belief.

INFLUENCE OF THE MIND ON THE IMMUNE SYSTEM

For a long time there has been a suspicion that mental factors could modify the function of the immune system, thereby having an effect on infectious processes, allergic reactions and cancer, among other factors harmful to the body. An important article appeared in the journal *Science* in April 1982 describing an experiment in which cancerous tumors were implanted into a population of rats.[3] The animals were then divided into three groups, one group receiving a series of electric shocks from which they could not escape, the second exposed to shocks but with the means of escaping the shock and the third group receiving no shock.

The article's authors found that only 27 percent of the rats receiving inescapable shock rejected the cancer, whereas 63 percent of the rats receiving escapable shock and 54 percent receiving no shock rejected the tumors. They concluded: "These results imply that lack of control over stressors reduces tumor rejection and decreases survival." If emotions can affect the rat immune system, they must surely do so in human beings as well. It is possible that herein lies the explanation for many of the unexplained examples of recovery from cancer recorded in the literature.

The examples of mind-body interaction presented here are small samples of evidence accumulating in the medical and lay literature attesting to the healing power of the mind. The introduction to Norman Cousins' book *Anatomy of an Illness* was written by the late Dr. René Jules Dubos, a world-famous medical scientist who participated in some of the most fundamental medical discoveries of this century. In his later years Dr. Dubos is quoted as having said, "I have an enormous belief that practically everything in the body is governed by the mind, that the mind is much more important than anything else in the body."[4]

Without a conscious attempt to follow any particular medical philosophy, my experience in the diagnosis and treatment of TMS resulted in ideas similar to those of Dr. Dubos. I learned from observing patients that if they could be liberated from the misconceptions and fears that characterize the conventional diagnoses and treatment of back pain, they would get better and stay better. Here was a clear example of biological resiliency, of the ability of the mind to create the conditions for recovery of the body by providing it with correct information. This, then, became the focus of treatment, the cornerstone of which might be called knowledge therapy.

KNOWLEDGE THERAPY

As stated earlier, a placebo works at an unconscious level, depending on "blind faith." What I discovered was that faith or belief in a concept could have a powerful, permanent therapeutic effect *if it was based on accurate information*. When patients were taught the facts of the tension myositis syndrome, they were able to develop confidence in the diagnosis; it made sense to them; they believed it at a *conscious* level. In a sense, I made my patients partners in the diagnostic process. "This is how it works," I said. "Do you agree?"

I found that patients who were able to say "yes" to that question got better—*without* a recurrence of their pain. I think the conscious belief became internalized, came to be accepted at an unconscious level, and as it did, the pain gradually disappeared. Occasionally it happened quickly, in a matter of days. I concluded that the unconscious acceptance of an idea is similar to the placebo reaction, with the important difference that the result appears to be permanent when the belief is based on a logical, rational concept.

I came to recognize this slowly, but it eventually became so obvious and worked so consistently that I decided to institute an educational process to be sure that patients had an ample opportunity to learn about TMS; hence the practice of inviting each patient to four hours of lecture-discussions. Eventually the invitation became a prescription.

It is surely a very strange kind of treatment to invite a group of patients to a lecture and proceed to teach them about their medical condition. People are accustomed to going to the doctor, being examined, told what they've got and given a prescription. They are passive recipients of treatment administered by their "omniscient" doctors but are not expected to participate in their own recovery except to follow instructions. This attitude is pervasive in Western society because the medical profession has fostered it. It is a natural consequence of failing to recognize the therapeutic potential of the patient's mind.

Recovery from TMS depends on an active patient who feels knowledgeable and confident. There are no formulas, magic pills, incantations, ritualized exercise routines or new technological gimmicks. Patients need to know what is causing the pain, what is not causing pain and that they have it within themselves to reverse the process that afflicts them. One might say, therefore, that changing patients' attitudes is the main job of the doctor who treats TMS. This is a first-rate challenge to the medical profession because it will require a drastic change in its own attitudes before it can hope to inculcate the proper ones in its patients.

The following case history illustrates the crucial importance of the patient's attitude.

The patient was a thirty-five-year-old married professional woman who had been having symptoms of low back and leg pain for a number of months. She was seen by the usual specialists and shortly before her appointment with me was advised to have surgery. She came to me at the suggestion of a physician relative who hoped that an operation could be avoided.

Both historically and on physical examination she had the classic symptoms of TMS—tenderness on both sides of the midline in virtually all the postural muscles from the neck to the buttocks. I suggested that this was the source of her pain and that the demonstrated herniated disc was incidental. It was clear when she left my office that she was skeptical of this diagnosis, but she agreed to go ahead with the program—that is, she started physical therapy and planned to attend the lectures. During the two weeks between the consultation and the lectures she continued to doubt the diagnosis, and there was no change in her pain syndrome.

An important element in this patient's history is that she lived outside New York City and was unable to come into the city for treatment. The physical therapist to whom I sent her in her home community had been trained at the Institute of Rehabilitation Medicine at New York University Medical Center and I discussed the diagnosis with him, hoping that his treatments would be helpful despite his lack of experience with TMS. He told me later that he, too, doubted the correctness of the diagnosis. However, he agreed to attend the lectures along with the patient, and apparently the evidence I presented convinced them both that the diagnosis was accurate. Armed with this confidence, they went back to work and over the next few weeks the pain gradually and progressively disappeared. A few weeks later she resumed playing tennis and as of this writing has remained free of symptoms.

The point is clear: As long as she doubted the diagnosis she could not bring her own inherent powers to bear on the process. She feared that there was a serious structural disorder of the spine that was causing the pain and that only some sort of intervention from the outside could correct the situation. When she came to understand and accept the fact that TMS was the cause of the pain, lost her fear of a structural abnormality and became confident in her own ability to participate in treatment, she recovered rapidly.

Through a process of trial and error I have gradually worked out the details of what must be taught to patients to develop the confidence necessary to throw off the symptoms of TMS. The teaching begins in my office at the time of the consultation, is continued in the formal lecture-discussions and reinforced by the physical therapist who administers physical treatment. A well-trained physical therapist can be very important to a successful outcome, for he or she can answer many of the patient's questions as treatment progresses. Most patients are initially very fearful, for they have been taught that their backs are weak and unstable, and they have experienced sudden, unexpected attacks of severe pain often associated with some physical incident or maneuver. A knowledgeable physical therapist can slowly build up patients' confidence by reassuring them that there is no structural problem and reminding them of the physiologic reason for the pain at any given moment.

Certain physical therapeutic measures are routinely ordered because of their local value. There are machines capable of warming the involved muscles and nerves, thereby increasing the local circulation by opening up the constricted blood vessels. Massage and exercise do the same thing, and all three of these treatments are generally prescribed. By increasing the local circulation the pain is substantially reduced or eliminated, an effect that sometimes persists for hours. This has a positive effect on the patient's outlook and can reinforce what is being taught about the cause of the pain. It is emphasized that pain from structural abnormalities, such as herniated discs, could not possibly be relieved by the application of these treatments.

The negative aspect of physical therapy in the treatment of TMS is that some patients may decide that physical measures, particularly the exercises, are the answer to the problem of TMS. This is true of those patients who are reluctant to accept the fact that tension is behind the disorder and who would rather believe that strengthening their muscles and the regular, disciplined performance of exercise will protect them from pain. Among this group are those, men primarily, who have an almost religious devotion to exercise. Though I think exercise is extremely important, it is essential to recognize its limitations. It will not eliminate or protect from TMS. As stated earlier, some patients have a placebo response to physical treatment, which means that they will have a recurrence of the pain.

Exercise is one of the most widely used treatments for back pain, but its role has never been properly understood. In our program the physical therapist uses it to increase local circulation, to stretch tight, contracted muscles and to increase physical well-being. Strengthening back and abdominal muscles does not diminish TMS per se, but it does restore patients' confidence in themselves as physical beings. Most patients need a knowledgeable person working with them physically during the weeks that the pain is resolving; the physical therapist fills that role admirably. The therapist can encourage, reassure, advise and explain. Patients often lapse into old habits of attributing pain to certain movements, positions, etc., during the course of the therapy. By correcting these habits and reinforcing the concepts of TMS the physical therapist makes a contribution to the recovery process.

As the pain gradually resolves, it is routine to recommend more vigorous physical activities. For some patients this means the resumption of things they did before, such as jogging, bicycle riding or tennis. Others need to be encouraged to introduce new activities. Aerobic exercise is important for everyone. Not only is it good for cardiovascular conditioning and general well-being, but also it is an excellent way to burn off excess tension. Elderly patients are advised to take brisk walks or swim. This is another role for the physical therapist: to assist patients in the choice and timing of these activities.

Therapists usually teach relaxation techniques, but I do not emphasize the value of such techniques in the treatment of TMS for the same reason that I advise patients not to be carried away by the importance of exercise. These can only be adjuncts at best; they will not make a substantial contribution to the elimination of TMS, as will knowledge, awareness and acceptance.

How does one teach awareness and acceptance? The latter sounds a little like a camp meeting with doctor as preacher exhorting the congregation to abandon sin and follow the true way. It is this element of belief that perplexes and bothers both patients and doctors, most particularly the latter, for they believe it is unscientific. Science to most doctors is equated with what is known as the scientific method, which is based primarily on the use of experiments. The use of the scientific method is responsible for much of what we know about physics, chemistry and biology today. But science is larger than the scientific method, for many situations in nature resist experimentation. In these cases one must depend upon deductions from the facts at hand to arrive at a theory.

Benjamin Franklin once wrote, "Nor is it of much Importance to us to know the Manner in which Nature executes her Laws; tis enough to know the Laws themselves."[5] A follow-up study, reported near the end of this chapter, revealed that the majority of treated patients recovered completely. Since acceptance of the diagnosis was the major thrust of treatment, it is logical to assume that this was the key to recovery.

Acceptance of the diagnosis depends on the doctor's ability to convince the patient that TMS is logical—more logical, in fact, than the structural diagnosis that the patient has heard in other doctors' offices. And so a great deal of time is devoted to the physiological and psychological details of TMS. But logic is intellectual, a function of the rational, conscious mind. Another part of the mind also demands satisfaction—the realm of unconscious emotion. It is there that feelings of apprehension, intimidation, victimization and helplessness reside, all of which are experienced by patients with well-established back pain problems.

It must be an almost universal human experience to feel that we are subject to illness or disease through forces completely outside our control. Upon becoming aware of pain, the usual reaction is to wonder where it came from and to worry about its seriousness. Those of us who have anxious personalities immediately think about cancer or some other serious disease. But the most destructive feelings are those of helplessness and victimization. Since we usually do not know the source of the trouble and have no idea that we can do anything about it, these are natural feelings.

Ironically, these feelings are inadvertently reinforced by contemporary Western medical philosophy, which holds that illness is an aberration in the body machinery and that it is the role of medicine to fix it. People look to the medical profession to deliver them from the throes of illness, of which they feel they are helpless victims.

This structural-mechanistic philosophy of medical practice is unfortunate; patients see themselves as passive recipients of whatever fate brings. They are not taught that nature has provided us with the mechanism to heal ourselves in many cases and that we need only learn how to work that mechanism.

As I looked at a scar forming on the back of my hand one day I reflected on the incredible ways of nature, how a disruption in the skin starts up a series of processes we call healing, with a variety of chemical and physical happenings, all of which eventuate in a new layer of skin over the injured area. It's all automatic; we don't have to do a thing about it. One wonders about the forces that created this situation and marvels at the ineluctable systems for self-restoration that are built into all living things.

This drive or force for self-restoration and self-healing operates if we will give it a chance. Modern human beings have lost sight of this, seeing themselves as helpless victims of whatever Fate brings. They are unaware of the powerful force for self-healing that exists within each of us. They have learned to feel as though "salvation" comes through the medical profession, that modern medical technology can solve all problems and eventually eliminate all disorders.

In our therapeutic program we allow the self-restorative process to function. By teaching that the source of pain is a benign muscle disorder related to tension, we make patients aware that they can modify this. That frees the body to heal itself. In taking away the fear, confusion and feelings of victimization so characteristic of TMS, we give the body a chance to do "its own thing."

Tension is a mental phenomenon. If a brain process such as tension can induce a painful condition in the muscles, it makes sense that some other brain process, such as learning the truth of the condition, can stop the painful condition.

These are, of course, speculations. Contemporary knowledge of brain physiology is rudimentary, and it may be a long time before we understand how nature executes its laws. Until then we must be content with accurate recognition of the laws that govern back pain and help patients to use the knowledge to rid themselves of the problem.

Is there a place for drugs in the treatment of TMS? The subject has already been discussed in Chapter 2, since drugs are so widely used in the conventional treatment of back pain. In the treatment of TMS, two classes of medication are occasionally used: "pain-killers" and tranquilizers. Neither is used as a cure, but each is employed to reduce pain or anxiety while the patient is following a program to get at the root of the problem. Both are reserved for patients with severe symptoms. Incidentally, neither "pain-killers" nor tranquilizers eliminate the pain or anxiety completely, in my experience. With these ground rules in mind I often use strong analgesics, including narcotics.

A well-known student of pain, Dr. H. K. Beecher, reported a clinical experience he had during World War II that has now become well known and often quoted in medical circles.[6] Dr. Beecher questioned 215 badly wounded soldiers at various locations in the European theater about their need for morphine shortly after having been wounded. He found that 75 percent of them had so little pain that they refused injections of morphine. Reflecting that strong emotion can block pain, Dr. Beecher went on to speculate, "In this connection it is important to consider the position of the soldier: His wound suddenly releases him from an exceedingly dangerous environment, one filled with fatigue, discomfort, anxiety, fear and real danger of death, and gives him a ticket to the safety of the hospital. His troubles are over, or he thinks they are."

This suggests that the severity and tolerability of pain depends very much on the patient's emotional state. If the person in pain is at the same time frightened, depressed, angry or frustrated, the pain will be more severe. If the patient has a hopeless feeling about what is causing the pain or is confused and worried about where the pain is coming from, it will be more severe. On the other hand, if the patient is joyful, as were some of the soldiers interviewed by Dr. Beecher, or is feeling calm about the medical reason behind the pain, it will be much more bearable.

It is my impression that "pain-killing" drugs improve the patient's mood rather than take away the pain. In other words, they act like efficient tranquilizers, making the pain bearable but not eliminating it. Someone who has just received morphine is likely to say, "I still have the pain but it doesn't bother me." If this is true it suggests that narcotics, which are the best "pain-killers," are really very superior tranquilizers. This is why they are effective for people in pain and probably why they are the most common addictive drugs of people without pain. They are the best substances around for making people "feel good," whether they are having pain or not.

I have often said that if heroin were legally available in this country, as it is in England, I would use it in the treatment of patients with acute, severe pain, since I think it would do the job better than any other legally available drug. This often shocks people, since we have such a strong association of heroin with drug addiction. But any drug can be abused; it probably happens with heroin so often because the drug is so effective.

These observations have been very important in the treatment of patients with severe, chronic back pain syndromes. It has permitted me to use the best drugs available for relieving severe pain, without fear of addiction. Someone who is having a lot of pain can tolerate a dose of morphine that would induce coma in a "pain-free" person. This is no doubt because the individual with a great deal of pain also has a great deal of anxiety; the anxiety is repressed by the drug, rather than the pain.

Aside from analgesics and occasionally tranquilizers, I use no other drugs to treat TMS. In fact, if the pharmaceutical industry were to introduce a drug totally specific and effective for TMS, I would not use it. Whether it worked on the muscle or on the anxiety, it could not cure the disorder. It would lull patients into a false sense of security and take away all motivation to get at the root of the problem. The pain would be eliminated and patients would be delighted; but as soon as the drug was discontinued, the pain would return. In this instance a "wonder drug" for TMS would be counter to the patient's best interests by interfering with the educational process.

In the final analysis the treatment of TMS is primarily an exercise in preventive medicine. A permanent "cure" for TMS requires that the patient understand what it is, how it works and develops the confidence that through this understanding the process will cease. No drug will accomplish that.

The preventive medicine concept in the treatment of TMS is valid. We have postulated that if the "cure" is genuine it will be permanent, and follow-up studies have verified this. If patients have a significant recurrence of pain it means that the old concepts are still operative, which in turn indicates one of two things: The patient never accepted the TMS diagnosis, or despite acceptance of the diagnosis the amount of tension is so great that other measures are required to reduce it.

Fortunately, only a small number of patients fall into these categories. If it is a problem of nonacceptance and the patient is willing, there are further consultations and sometimes more lectures. In either category, psychotherapy may be indicated.

The need for psychotherapy is no disgrace, though there are still social taboos surrounding it, especially for older generations. Many of us carry attitudes developed in childhood into our adult life. We may be totally unaware of them until they surface in response to the vicissitudes of life. For example, behind hardworking, compulsive traits there may be feelings of inferiority. The result of this is a great deal of tension, which may then lead to TMS. When such inner problems exist, the individual must be made aware of them, for recognition usually leads to a reduction in tension and, in turn, resolution of the pain.

One of the most common and most natural questions patients ask is, "How long will it take for the pain to go away?" In my experience, the usual range is from four to eight weeks from the time the diagnosis is made; in a few it will be a shorter period; in some others, longer. I find it remarkable that it can happen as quickly as it does, especially in those who have had the problem for many years. In our follow-up study we found that the average duration of symptoms in the 177 patients surveyed was eight years, with some having histories of pain for fifteen years or more. Yet even in the long-term patients the pain could leave in a matter of weeks. This rapid effect cannot be explained with certainty, but I suspect it is because patients need only understand and accept the diagnosis of TMS rather than effect basic personality or life changes.

On the other hand, if all that is necessary is to understand and accept, why does it take from four to eight weeks? Some patients accept the diagnosis immediately, finding it very logical and consistent. Accepting something in one's conscious mind does not mean that it has been accepted in the unconscious mind. That part of the mind is much slower to accept new ideas, new thoughts, but it will do so if one works at it and is clear about what's going on; if there are doubts, they must be resolved. The lecture-discussions are helpful in this regard; patients ask questions and get clarifying answers. Often other patients volunteer experiences and thoughts that help to make a point.

Over the four- to eight-week period I believe that the new ideas slowly penetrate the unconscious mind, which is where TMS originates, and as it does, there is gradual disappearance of the pain.

Though the majority of patients become symptom-free in this period, some require a number of months before the process comes under good control. This is the result of psychological factors that cannot be described here adequately. Such patients may have an excellent response in four to eight weeks but then develop other manifestations of TMS a few weeks or months later, usually in association with an emotionally charged situation. When this occurs it is of primary importance to ascertain the patient's ideas about the cause of the pain. Does the patient think it is due to TMS? Does he or she recognize the role of tension in precipitating the return of pain? Because of the change in symptoms, did he or she attribute the pain to a structural abnormality? When the location or pattern of pain changes, patients are strongly inclined to attribute it to a structural problem and need reassurance that it is simply another of the many faces of TMS.

I recall a man who had an excellent result with initial treatment and resumed running after many years of disabling back and leg pain. A few months later he developed pain in one of his knees, and though he protested that he was totally convinced that his previous back pain had been due to TMS, he was worried about this new symptom. After an examination and discussion we decided that he should continue to run, and eventually the knee pain disappeared. Not long after, he developed a recurrence of back spasm, but this time it was clearly related to a psychologically disturbing event in his life and was short-lived. With each of these experiences his confidence in the idea of TMS increased, as did his realization that he had a very strong tendency to express tension physically. I have followed this patient's progress closely; he continues to have some low back pain much of the time, but it is mild and does not prevent him from running many miles each week. He is leading a normal, unrestricted life.

If a patient has a rapid and complete resolution of symptoms in a few days I suspect a placebo reaction. This is not acceptable because the placebo effect is temporary, and it is our goal to bring about a permanent resolution of the problem. Only patients with a very short, mild history will get better legitimately in just a few days.

The best support for TMS treatment described in this book is to be found in the results of treatment. The following statistics demonstrate that the majority of patients have been treated successfully.

During the summer of 1982 a telephone survey was conducted in which 177 TMS patients were questioned about the results of their treatment. Their names were chosen consecutively by a research assistant and my secretary from my appointment book and a roster of patients who had been referred to one specific physical therapist. The latter strategy was adopted to compare the results of treatment with one particular therapist as opposed to random referral to a variety of other physical therapists. (We found no difference in outcome with these two groups.)

All patients in the survey were diagnosed by me as having TMS. Each one had been referred with some structural diagnosis, the most common being herniated lumbar disc, lumbar osteoarthritis, cervical (neck) disc disease and cervical osteoarthritis. Every patient was instructed as to the nature of TMS; most attended lectures, though some had been treated prior to the time lectures were instituted. Most of the patients had a course of physical therapy.

The group ranged in age from fifteen to seventy-seven years, with 79 percent between the ages of thirty and fifty-nine. There were ninety-five men and eighty-two women. The duration of back pain was from one month to forty-two years, with a median of five years and an average of eight years. These figures indicate that we were not dealing with patients who had recent, mild problems; the majority were hard-core back pain sufferers who had tried a variety of treatments without lasting benefit.

To demonstrate the permanence of treatment results, no patient was included whose treatment had concluded less than a year before the survey. The actual range of time elapsed since completion of treatment was twelve to forty-two months.

The statistical outcome speaks for itself (see Figure 10). A total of 76 percent were relieved of significant pain, 62 percent were totally relieved (Group A) and 14 percent (Group B) had minor recurrences of no importance—that is, the discomfort was

Figure 10

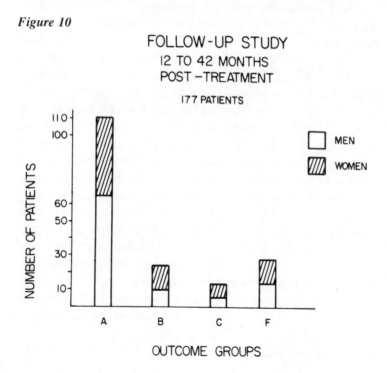

FOLLOW-UP STUDY
12 TO 42 MONTHS
POST-TREATMENT

177 PATIENTS

MEN
WOMEN

NUMBER OF PATIENTS

OUTCOME GROUPS

mild, transient and did not prohibit even the most vigorous physical activity. Fourteen patients (Group C) were improved to varying degrees, and only twenty-eight patients, or 16 percent, were treatment failures (Group F). The latter were questioned closely; the majority did not accept the diagnosis of TMS. A disproportionate number of this group was in the older age range (sixty to seventy-seven years of age).

The successfully treated patients were living normal lives with no physical restrictions; most were engaged in aerobic exercise and/or vigorous sports such as tennis, jogging, or skiing.

CHRONIC PAIN

There is another message in this book; it concerns the problem of *chronic pain*. Many people in the United States are no longer able to hold jobs or function as homemakers because of chronic pain. The majority are supported by workers' compensation, other insurance or Social Security benefits; some are on welfare. These people have been through the medical system and emerged with intractable, disabling pain. Many have had surgery, often multiple, and a host of other treatments. Although the majority have been managed with care and sensitivity, some have been accused of malingering or mental illness and discarded as hopeless.

One of the significant medical responses to this great problem has been the development of "pain clinics" all over the United States, primarily in teaching medical centers and large community hospitals. These clinics bring together many medical and paramedical disciplines that employ both physical and psychological treatment. The guiding therapeutic principles of most of them are based on the concept that chronic pain is a separate disease entity. They believe that there is a residual structural abnormality causing the pain and that patients who become disabled by this pain have unconsciously learned to derive some benefit from it. These include such things as financial gain, escape from the drudgery of work, and the care and attention of family and friends. Following behavioral psychological tenets their treatment is designed to help patients "unlearn" these habits and substitute healthier attitudes toward their pain.

I consider this approach to chronic pain to be fundamentally erroneous. There are two major fallacies in its conceptualization:

1. There is an underlying structural disorder that represents the basis for continuing pain.
2. This pain is perpetuated and aggravated by an unconscious desire for "secondary gain."

My disagreement with both of these ideas is rooted in my experience with patients who have chronic back pain. Since 1974 my staff and I have carried on an inpatient program to treat these patients at the Institute of Rehabilitation Medicine. We have concluded that:

1. There is no underlying structural disorder in the majority of these patients; most of them suffer from TMS, which is physical but not structural, a central tenet of this book.
2. "Secondary gain" is not the motivating psychological force behind the pain syndrome but anxiety, depression and psychological conflict. "Secondary gain" undoubtedly exists but represents a small part of the psychological process and should not be the major thrust of psychotherapy.

On the basis of my experience with the entire spectrum of patients with TMS, from the mildest to the most severe, I find that the concept of "behavioral pain" is degrading and, in the long run, destructive. It leads patients to believe that though the motives may be unconscious, they really want the pain, that "they have done it to themselves." I have heard patients express this sentiment with great bitterness and sadness. In fact, they often react to the initial diagnosis of the tension myositis syndrome in this way and must be immediately reassured that the process is not the result of a hidden desire to be in pain. Back pain patients (people with TMS) are already guilt-ridden and overly conscientious; the additional burden of being told that they are responsible for their pain only increases their anxiety.

The concept of "behavioral pain" became even more unconvincing when I realized how the medical system creates and reinforces the idea in patients' minds that their backs are ruined, fragile structures. The patient thinks, "I have had the best treatment medicine has to offer and since I'm not better something must be terribly wrong." Simultaneously, the system generates great fear. I recall a woman who became terrified when she read in a well-known book on the back that if you had a mildly herniated disc and became active too soon it would fully herniate and then require surgery. Another patient was told by the doctor as she left the hospital after refusing surgery, "You will be back in two weeks screaming in pain and begging me for an operation." These are only two among many examples of how the medical system helps perpetuate the problem of tension myositis by frightening patients. Anxiety and fear are the perpetuators of back pain, not "secondary gain."

In my view, the behaviorist concept of chronic pain is based upon a lack of knowledge of both the psychology and physiology of these pain syndromes. I fear it will be many years before the negative effects of this theory are reversed.

The inpatient program at the Institute of Rehabilitation Medicine for the treatment of patients disabled by chronic back pain incorporates all the therapeutic modalities described above except that they are applied more intensively than for outpatients. Three or four patients are treated simultaneously, bringing benefits in the camaraderie and opportunity to share experiences, clarify concepts and support each other.

I spend the first hour of each day with the group teaching the concepts of TMS and meeting with them individually to discuss personal problems. They have either group or individual psychotherapy each day of the week. There is also daily individual or group physical and occupational therapy designed to increase mobility and flexibility, apply specific modalities to increase local blood circulation and generally restore their confidence in themselves as competent physical beings. For those who need them, social and vocational services are available.

Pain is discussed openly and freely so that patients can learn to identify it as a manifestation of tension. They are encouraged to "think psychologically." Doing so, they learn to correlate increases in pain with emotional rather than physical phenomena.

Medications are administered as needed but, contrary to behaviorist practices, patients are partners with me in the decision-making process. When pain diminishes they usually reject medication spontaneously. When drugs are requested despite reduced pain, it is taken as evidence that the patient is psychologically dependent on them; this then becomes an issue to be dealt with in psychotherapy.

CASE HISTORY

The following case history illustrates what is done in the inpatient program.

The patient was a forty-four-year-old woman who had her first attack of back pain at age twenty-five. Eight years before I saw her, she developed numbness in the left leg, and about a year later she had back surgery. There was no relief from the pain. A year after that a second operation was performed, again without benefit, followed thirteen months later by a spinal fusion, to no avail. The pain persisted virtually unchanged, and she remained quite disabled. About two years before her first visit with me a CT scan was done; she was told there was nothing structurally wrong with the spine and that the pain probably was due to "scar tissue." She was advised that she would have to learn to live with it. Gradually she became "addicted" to a narcotic.

The extent of the patient's disability can be partially discerned by the fact that she was a college-educated pianist, accompanist and piano teacher but was unable to play or teach because she could not sit. She was married and the mother of two adopted children. Most homemaking chores were impossible for her. The limitations imposed by pain adversely affected her relationship with her husband and children. To avoid lying at home on a couch all day she took a job at a local bank.

When I first saw the patient she was having almost constant pain in the low back and left buttock, radiating into the left leg, associated primarily with activity but also aggravated by sitting and standing in one place. The pain usually got worse as the day wore on.

On physical examination she was basically normal except that the tendon reflex at the left ankle was absent, the left leg seemed generally weak and there was marked tenderness on pressure over the muscles of the neck, shoulders, low back and buttocks on both sides. The history and physical findings were typical of TMS.

As we came to know the patient it was apparent that she possessed many of the traits characteristic of women with severe TMS. She was compulsive, perfectionistic and prone to put the needs of others before her own, particularly those of her family. She was plagued with self-doubt and generally lacked confidence in herself, though she was clearly very intelligent and talented. There was evidence of underlying anger.

In her characteristic fashion the patient entered into the program with energy and enthusiasm. The realization that the pain was not structural came as an important revelation to her, following which she was able to focus on the psychotherapeutic process. Slowly she began to acknowledge long-suppressed feelings and recognize the meanings behind her various personality traits. As she delved more deeply into these psychological matters we witnessed a striking transformation: Physical mobility returned to normal; the pain gradually diminished; at about the sixth week she discontinued the narcotic on her own, with no untoward physical reaction. By discharge she was virtually free of pain.

It is not difficult to imagine the patient's reaction to this experience. Her own words describe it best:

> The ten weeks I spent at the Institute of Rehabilitation Medicine were at the least remarkable. With the help of intensive physical therapy and psychotherapy, along with a thorough reeducation from Dr. Sarno, my life is no longer a circle with no options ahead of me. Rather, I am back in the mainstream of activity, functioning at full capacity with no medication, and with a whole series of highways before me, none of which have dead ends! I am resuming my career in music—accompanying and teaching piano—an option I did not have prior to this. My family enjoys my laughter, something I discovered I had been without for many years. In fact, it is revealing to me that it is not only I who have benefited from my IRM stay, but my husband and two teenage children are radiant and blossoming as well.

Naturally, this case history was chosen because of the patient's excellent, rapid response to treatment. Not all patients do so well. In many cases there is still pain at discharge, and physical therapy and psychotherapy are continued on an outpatient basis. Some fail completely. The overall results are generally good. In 1976 I published a paper in the *Scandinavian Journal of Rehabilitation Medicine* describing our experience with the first twenty-eight patients treated in the program. Sixty-eight percent were discharged free of pain or sufficiently improved to permit normal activity. Long-term follow-up revealed that 64 percent remained in those categories. Twenty-one percent derived some improvement from the program; 11 percent showed no change.[7]

I have tried to convey in this chapter the principles and practices that led to our treatment results. It is difficult to make them clear, for we are dealing with a subject that is abstract and about which we are not accustomed to thinking.

Fundamental to understanding the diagnosis and treatment of TMS is the fact that the mind and body are inseparable and interactive. For this reason a study of human physiology and illness is incomplete unless it includes the role of the mind. Conversely, the study of mental illness must take into account the influence of the body on the mind. Failure to apply this principle has been responsible for much diagnostic and therapeutic confusion; the neck and back pain syndromes are good examples. They are by no means unique.

In my judgment, our diagnosis and treatment of TMS represent yet another instance of what is possible when the power of the mind is mobilized for healing the body. It is not magic; it is as scientific as the appropriate use of antibiotics, for science encompasses everything that is true in nature. We must learn to recognize nature's truths even though we don't understand them, for some of those truths may still be beyond the ability of the human mind to comprehend. What we need is a compound prescription of humility, imagination, devotion to the truth and, above all, confidence in the eternal wisdom of nature.

Coda

At the completion of this book I feel compelled to add a word about where my experience with back pain fits in the contemporary medical scene. What kind of medicine does it represent?

There is probably no other medical condition which is treated in so many different ways and by such a variety of practitioners as back pain. Though the conclusion may be uncomfortable, the medical community must bear the responsibility for this, for it has been distressingly narrow in its approach to the problem. It has been trapped by a diagnostic bias of ancient vintage and, most uncharacteristically, has uncritically accepted an unproven concept, that structural abnormalities are the cause of back pain. The resulting inability to diagnose properly and treat this disorder has driven patients to seek help outside the boundaries of conventional medicine.

Is my diagnosis and treatment of back pain an example of holistic medicine? The avowed philosophy of those who practice holistic medicine is to look at and treat the whole man, meaning the emotional as well as the physical man. But a famous British physician of the nineteenth century, Sir William Osler, often referred to as the father of modern medicine, frequently pointed out the importance of emotional factors in physical illness. However, many medical scientists of the twentieth century, intoxicated by the laboratory, apparently have forgotten the teachings of their distinguished predecessors and approach the diagnosis and treatment of illness as though humans were a kind of complex machine and one need only understand the physics and chemistry of the body to solve all medical problems.

On the other side of the coin, these same medical scientists tend to draw a sharp line between physical and psychological phenomena, as though there were no connection between the two. The back pain epidemic is a good example of what can happen in that kind of medical climate.

Given this situation, it was inevitable that doctors would try to redress the wrong; hence, the holistic medicine movement. Unfortunately, some of the proponents of holistic medicine are less than objective in their approach to medical problems, so we are left no closer to correct solutions.

In my view there is no need for such a movement. All doctors should be practitioners of holistic medicine in the sense that they recognize the interaction between mind and body. To leave the emotional dimension out of the study of illness demonstrates a bias and is, therefore, poor science.

My work is not an example of holistic medicine. Its conclusions are based on observation verified by experience. Though the cause of TMS is tension, the diagnosis is made on physical and not psychological grounds, in the tradition of clinical medicine.

In another tradition, that of scientific medicine, I invite my colleagues to verify or correct my work. What they may not do is ignore it, for the problem of back pain is too great and the need for a solution is imperative.

Notes

Introduction

1. M.V. Gilberti, "Dilemmas of the Occupational Physician in Assessing Low Back Pain," *Occupational Medicine Current Concepts*, Vol. 5 (Spring 1982).

2. H.G. Fassbender and K. Wegner, "Morphologie und Pathogenese des Weichteilrheumatismus," *Z. Rheumaforsch*, Vol. 32 (1973), p. 355.

Chapter 1

1. J.E. Sarno, "Etiology of Neck and Back Pain: An Autonomic Myoneuralgia?" *The Journal of Nervous and Mental Disease*, Vol. 169 (1981), p. 55.

2. J.E. Sarno, "Therapeutic Exercise for Back Pain," *Therapeutic Exercise*, 4th ed., ed. J.V. Basmajian (Baltimore: Williams & Wilkins, in press).

3. A.J. Fox, J.P. Lin, R.S. Pinto, et al., "Myelographic Cervical Nerve Root Deformities," *Radiology*, Vol. 116 (1975), p. 355.

4. C.A. Splithoff, "Lumbosacral Junction Roentgenographic Comparison of Patients with and Without Backaches," *Journal of the American Medical Association*, Vol. 152 (1953), p. 1610.

5. A. Magora and A. Schwartz, "Relation Between the Low Back Pain Syndrome and X-Ray Findings. 1. Degenerative Osteoarthritis," *Scandinavian Journal of Rehabilitation Medicine*, Vol. 8 (1976), p. 115.

6. A. Magora and A. Schwartz, "Relation Between the Low Back Pain Syndrome and X-Ray Findings. 2. Transitional Vertebra (Mainly Sacralization)," *Scandinavian Journal of Rehabilitation Medicine,* Vol. 10 (1978), p. 135.

7. A. Magora and A. Schwartz, "Relation Between the Low Back Pain Syndrome and X-Ray Findings. 3. Spina Bifida Occulta," *Scandinavian Journal of Rehabilitation Medicine,* Vol. 12 (1980), p. 9.

8. A. Magora and A. Schwartz, "Relation Between Low Back Pain and X-Ray Changes. 4. Lysis and Olisthesis," *Scandinavian Journal of Rehabilitation Medicine,* Vol. 12 (1980), p. 47.

Chapter 2
1. G. Thorsteinsson, H.H. Stonnington, G.K. Stillwell and L.R. Elveback, "The Placebo Effects of Transcutaneous Electrical Stimulation," *Pain,* Vol. 5 (1975), p. 31.

2. A.L. Nachemson, "The Lumbar Spine: An Orthopedic Challenge," *Spine,* Vol. 1 (1976), p. 59.

Chapter 3
1. M. Friedman and R.H. Rosenman, *Type A Behavior and Your Heart* (New York: Alfred A. Knopf, 1974).

2. K. Horney, *Neurosis and Human Growth,* Chap. 5 (New York: W.W. Norton, 1970).

3. R. Baker, "Where Have All the Ulcers Gone?" *The New York Times Magazine* (Aug. 16, 1981), p. 14.

4. M. Sargent, "Psychosomatic Backache," *New England Journal of Medicine,* Vol. 234 (1946), p. 427.

5. T.H. Holmes and H.G. Wolff, "Life Situations, Emotions and Backache," *Psychosomatic Medicine,* Vol. 14 (1974), p. 23.

Chapter 4
1. G.E. Robinson, "A Combined Approach to a Medical Problem: The Canadian Back Education Unit," *Canadian Journal of Psychiatry,* Vol. 24 (1980), p. 138.

Chapter 5
1. N. Cousins, *Anatomy of an Illness* (New York: W.W. Norton, 1979).

2. L.C. Whiton, "Under the Power of the Gran Gadu," *Natural History,* Vol. 80, No. 7 (Aug.–Sept. 1971).

3. M.A. Visintainer, J.R. Volpicelli, and M.E.P. Seligman, "Tumor Rejection in Rats After Inescapable or Escapable Shock" *Science,* Vol. 216 (1982), p. 437.

4. A.S. Freese, "Dubos at 80," *Modern Maturity* (Aug.–Sept. 1981).

5. C.D. Bowen, *The Most Dangerous Man in America* (Boston: Little, Brown & Company, 1974).

6. H.K. Beecher, "Pain in Men Wounded in Battle," *Annals of Surgery,* Vol. 123 (1946), p. 96.

7. J.E. Sarno, "Chronic Back Pain and Psychic Conflict," *Scandinavian Journal of Rehabilitation Medicine,* Vol. 8 (1976), p. 143.

Glossary

autonomic nervous system: That branch of the nervous system which controls involuntary functions such as digestion, circulation of the blood, urinary function, etc.

brachial plexus: The network of nerves located near the neck (one on each side) that divides into the nerves that go to the arms and hands.

CT scan: An X-ray technique using computer technology that supplies more detailed information than conventional X rays.

herniated disc: The condition that exists when some of the thick liquid in a disc ruptures through the wall of the disc.

ischemia: The condition in which some body tissue contains a less than normal supply of blood.

lumbar: The lowest part of the back, just above the buttocks.

pathology: The result of an abnormal process in the body; for example, an infection, an injury or an abnormal growth.

"pinched nerve": A nerve that is compressed, usually by bone.

placebo: Any form of treatment that has no inherent value but may nevertheless alleviate symptoms.

replication: Reproduction; usually used to refer to repeating an experiment and obtaining the same results.

sciatic nerve: The largest nerves in the body (one on each side); they begin in the buttocks and supply nerve function to most of each leg.

scoliosis: An abnormal curvature of the spine.

spina bifida occulta: A congenital abnormality of the lower end of the spine in which part of the bone is missing.

spondylolisthesis: An abnormality, usually at the lower end of the spine, in which a vertebra is not lined up correctly with the vertebra below it.

syndrome: A group of signs and symptoms that characterize an abnormal condition in the body.

tension myositis syndrome (TMS): A painful condition involving postural muscles and associated nerves caused by nervous tension.

transcutaneous nerve stimulation (TNS): A treatment for pain in which nerves are stimulated by mild electric shocks.

transitional vertebra: A congenital abnormality of the lower end of the spine in which there is an extra segment of bone.

vertebrae: The technical name for the bones of the spine.

Index